"It is a special treat to find a guide to Ser‑ beyond homilies and platitudes to address the now to real for the leader and their organization. A truly practical guide that deserves your time and attention!"

—Leonard A. Schlesinger, Baker Foundation Professor-Harvard Business School, President Emeritus-Babson College

"This book offers leaders five guiding principles to help them build an engaged workforce. The 'field guide, notes from the field' approach couples practical learnings from a Chief Human Resources Officer who has worked in three different industries, with a rich array of real world examples and stories. I've worked with the author, and I've seen first-hand that leaders at every level find the ideas contained in this book to be both thought provoking and inspiring."

—Ken Jennings PHD, Co-author of the international best selling book *The Serving Leader*, Principal Third River Partners

"Employee engagement is a huge worldwide challenge and Joe addresses it the way a servant-leader would, by focusing on and growing people. He presents a practical approach to create that change, showing real world examples and stories where it is work-ing in highly regarded workplaces. I strongly support his book and have applied it in my own work."

—Dr. Kent Keith, Author of *Anyway: The Paradoxical Commandments*, Former CEO of Robert Greenleaf Center for Servant Leadership, President of Pacific Rim Christian University

"This book delivers a fresh and powerful perspective by connecting em-ployee engagement with servant-leadership. It is an easy and interesting read, filled with thought provoking questions. The author's personal experience is credible. He shares examples, stories and the field book style is practical and hands-on. This book would be especially beneficial for leaders who have tried and are frustrated with previous attempts at building employee engagement."

—Linda Belton, MS, LFACHE, Director of Organizational Health (ret), National Center for Organization Development, Veterans Health Administration

"The author draws upon his own professional and personal experiences and those of others to offer meaningful insights into what it takes to achieve lasting organizational change. The core principles he lays out, the examples and research he draws upon, and the compelling stories, are presented in a way that a leader in any size organization will appreciate. This book will truly inspire people to transform their organizations and their lives."

—Leslie Leete Smith, M.B.A., Medical Practice Manager, Briarpatch Pediatrics, Olympian and Alpine World Cup Skier

"As the owner of a small business in an industry that is going through immense change, I'm always looking for ways to help the people in my organization bring their very best to everything that we do. The practical, powerful ideas in this book will definitely help me achieve that goal, and I know they will help other business leaders, in large companies or small. The book is also a very good read, filled with stories that are often as moving as they are useful. "

—Paul Mustone, CEO Reflex Lighting

"Building engaged work environments is Joe's passion, which he enthusiastically shares in this book through real world experiences and practical recommendations. It will inspire leaders at all levels to step up and create an environment that brings out the best in their people and their organization."

—Robert Gregorio, EVP & Chief Administrative Officer, Sunovion Pharmaceuticals Inc

THE ENGAGED
ENTERPRISE

A FIELD GUIDE FOR THE
SERVANT-LEADER

Book design by Adam Robinson

Published by The Greenleaf Center for Servant Leadership
133 Peachtree St. NE, Suite 350
Atlanta, GA 30303
www.greenleaf.org

THE ENGAGED ENTERPRISE

A FIELD GUIDE FOR THE SERVANT-LEADER

Bringing out the best in your people and your organization!

JOSEPH M. PATRNCHAK

This book is dedicated to all those who strive for excellence by "doing the ordinary things extraordinarily well." In doing so, you make the world a better place.

I thank you for your inspiration.

CONTENTS

ACKNOWLEDGEMENTS

THERE ARE SO MANY PEOPLE I NEED TO SHARE MY HEARTFELT thanks with … people without whom I'm certain this book would not have been written.

It's important for me to start with Jim McGovern. His research and writing skills have taken this book from a concept to a reality. To say he kept me honest and on track throughout this process is understatement for sure. His interest and thought leadership around this topic made it a fun, spirited process. Because of our friendship and trust, our conversations ranged over a number of diverse and meaningful topics, all of which added great value to the book. I'd like to think we learned a lot from each other.

To my late parents—my father Joseph, a steel worker, and my mother Lucy, a General Motors worker—who taught their children to value hard work and not be afraid of anything that took hard work. They taught us by example that there was dignity in all forms of work and especially in the people who did the work. I can't thank them enough.

The family background I grew up in has always been a source of strength for me. I owe so much of who I am to my sister Monica, a dedicated, talented educator; my late brother John, whom I loved for the 45 years of his life, and my late baby sister Mary Anne, whom I loved for the 6 months of her short life; and my identical twin brother Carl, with whom I have shared life since before we were born. To my nieces and nephews—Christine, Katie, Bobby, Natalie, Naomi, and Jimmy—who represent the next generation of workers: I've learned a lot from you. I don't think we need be concerned about the millennial workforce.

I'd also like to thank my extended family of cousins, aunts, and uncles—especially Edith and Carl Ritch, who have been great role models in all areas of life. They traveled around the country to watch Carl and me play football for Northwestern University, despite being diehard Ohio State fans!

And then there are all the friends and colleagues who provided valuable feedback as this book evolved. Dr. Ken Jennings, a leading author and consultant, who encouraged me to tell this story and was so generous with his advice. Peter Mercury, SVP and General Manager at Digital, Compaq, and HP, whom I loved working with and from whom I learned so much. Mary El'Hatton, whose comments as a former English teacher were so insightful, and whose husband, the late David El'Hatton, was my lifelong coach, friend, and mentor. Paul Mustone, CEO of Reflex Lighting, and my lifelong friend David Frazier, CEO of the Charles Manufacturing Company, two very successful entrepreneurs, provided great feedback and encouragement. To Father Bill Brown, my friend and spiritual advisor, I say thanks for your feedback and your prayers. And to Anila Nicklos, who emigrated from communist Albania in 1997: you've been an inspiration to me, and I'm fortunate to be your friend and God Parent.

Rebekah Burrows, a dedicated art therapist, helped capture what I was trying to communicate through her wonderful illustrations. Working with her was a great learning experience in itself! Rebekah, you do wonderful things to help people every day. Please continue to do that work and to be a blessing.

FOREWORD

I FIRST MET JOE PATRNCHAK SHORTLY AFTER HE LEFT HIS ROLE as the Chief Human Resources Officer at Cleveland Clinic to start his own firm, Green Summit Partners. The timing could not have been more perfect. A bank had just acquired my company, which I had successfully led for the last 20 years. The acquisition brought on a phase of great uncertainty.

I was concerned about our company culture and the entrepreneurial spirit that had driven its growth for years. I worried about how a highly regulated, much larger parent organization would affect our team and its relentless passion for our brand. At the same time, I knew there was a real opportunity to continue to grow and improve as both a team and business overall. While I didn't know how to answer all these concerns, I did know that a high level of employee engagement was the only way we could achieve our future potential.

So I took my executive team offsite, where Joe first led us through a thought provoking exercise to examine and develop our company purpose. With that under our belts, we worked on a plan to anchor our culture and significantly increase our employee engagement. As the day progressed, Joe led us through the five key principles in this book, at the center of which is the concept of Servant-Leadership.

My team left that retreat with a clear framework with which to take our company to the next level by anchoring our culture in Servant-Leadership. To some extent, Servant-Leadership was already part of our culture, although we didn't call it that, but with Joe's help we came to see that we had just scratched the surface of becoming Servant-Leaders. The framework helped us clearly differentiate the things we were doing that were highly effective from others that were not. That alone was a huge learning!

Building...and sustaining...an engaged enterprise is not easy; it requires fortitude and consistency. Mostly, it requires you as a leader to turn inward and commit to improving yourself by unleashing others. I fully endorse that the principles discussed in this book will help you create and execute a holistic plan to meet that challenge in the way that works best for your particular organization. It did for us and continues to do so.

Stories make it real, and Joe's book brings real life examples from an array of companies that demonstrate the principles he outlines and vividly illustrate Servant-Leadership in action. These *Notes from the Field* also come from Joe's own experience in three different industries, including a detailed description of what it took to transform Cleveland Clinic into a "great place to work and grow."

This book will leave you empowered and feeling inspired that you can take action within your own organization, no matter what leadership role you may have, no matter how large or small the organization. As a leader, we're all called to make a difference in people's lives. There's no better way to do that than by being a Servant-Leader and building an engaged enterprise that brings out the best in people.

James Broom
CEO, Direct Capital, A Division of CIT Bank

PROLOGUE

ENGAGEMENT ... WHAT'S
IT ALL ABOUT?

THIS BOOK IS ABOUT BUILDING AN ENGAGED ENTERPRISE. IT'S about what it takes—what kind of leadership it takes—to create high levels of employee engagement all across your organization, whether that organization is local or global, whether it consists of 50 people or 50,000 people.

What do we mean by engagement? Is it different from employee morale? Is it the same as, or different from, job satisfaction? Is it a set of beliefs that an employee holds or a set of behaviors that an employee demonstrates? Is it both?

Despite the 30+ years of research devoted to the subject of engagement, despite all the articles, books, and blogs on the subject by management consultants and gurus, there's no agreement on exactly what the term means. While it's also fair to say that most of us have an intuitive sense of what we mean by employee engagement, here's a definition that works for me:

> *Employee engagement is a heightened emotional and intellectual connection that an employee has to his/her job, organization, manager, or co-workers that, in turn, influences him/her to apply additional discretionary effort to his/her work*[1].

---

1 Gibbons J. *Employee engagement: a review of current research and its implications*. Conference Board; NY; 2006. Available at: http://montrealoffice. wikispaces.com/file/view/Employee+Engagement+-+Conference+Board. pdf.

I

While the language may be a little formal, this definition makes two key points: (1) engagement has both emotional and intellectual components, and (2) equally important, the combined result is extra on-the-job effort. But what does engagement actually look like in the real world?

> When was the last time you dealt with someone in your own organization who "applied extra discretionary effort to their work?"
>
> How about a similar experience outside your organization?
>
> In each case, how did you respond?

We've all experienced what it's like to deal with both engaged and disengaged employees. For example, when I created my personal website, a friend recommended GoDaddy as a service provider, because he said they had exceptional customer support. Since I'm not the most tech-savvy person around, that seemed important. Sure enough I wasn't very far into the process when I ran into problems. Enter "Olivia," a GoDaddy customer support rep.

Olivia couldn't have been friendlier, more responsive, or more professional. Very patiently, she took me through the necessary troubleshooting process, found the problem, and fixed it, without ever making me feel like a dunce. Two days later she sent me this e-mail:

> *I again want to thank you for your time and your business. Please feel free to email me anytime you have questions. I do have access to my email after hours, but please allow me some time to respond if I'm away from the office. I will be happy to call you back if you provide a call back number. Please let me know if I can help in any other way.*

Since then I've had occasion to reach out to Olivia several times for help with various issues, and she's always responded quickly and professionally. That's someone who is putting everything she has into the task at hand, and then giving just a bit more. That's what engagement looks like.

There's nothing dramatic about this example. There are more dramatic examples of employee engagement later in these pages, but I chose the story of Olivia because most of the time, in most organizations, engagement doesn't involve anything dramatic. Most of the time, engagement comes down to "ordinary" employees putting a little extra effort into "ordinary" everyday tasks.

One of my favorite poems is called "The Ordinary Caregiver." It opens with these lines:

Love
Is the greatest human virtue,
But is just ordinary love to one, who nurtures,
One who is just
An ordinary caregiver…

What the poem is saying is that the very term "ordinary caregiver" is an oxymoron, a contradiction in terms, because there is

Doing ordinary things extraordinarily well.

nothing ordinary about caring for others, even in the most seemingly ordinary ways. In fact, my personal definition of excellence is doing ordinary things extraordinarily well.

Imagine if you had 90% of all your employees doing ordinary things extraordinarily well what dramatic results you could achieve.

PUTTING IT ALL TOGETHER—
THE ENGAGED ORGANIZATION

How many engaged employees—how many Olivias—does it take to create an engaged organization?

The Gallup organization has studied engagement in companies across the world. According to their extensive body of research, it takes four engaged employees to offset the negative effect of just one actively disengaged employee, because those actively disengaged employees "aren't just unhappy at work; they're busy acting out their unhappiness. Every day these workers undermine what their engaged co-workers accomplish."

Think how toxic these actively disengaged employees are in your organization—how many extra meetings, how much wasted time and energy, how many workarounds it takes to get anything done in the face of their cynical attitude.

According to Gallup, in a world class organization the ratio of engaged to actively disengaged employees is 9.6 to 1. So let me ask you this. Based on what you see every day, would you say that 90% of the people around you have an emotional and intellectual connection to the organization and their job—a strong enough connection that they regularly put in extra effort to help the organization succeed? Is the number 50%? Could it be even less?

HOW MUCH DOES ENGAGEMENT MATTER?

The real question is: does engagement make a significant difference to an organization's day-to-day performance? It's great if employees feel an emotional connection to their work, especially if that means they put in some extra effort, but overall, does that make a difference?

The answer to that question is clear. These several

> In an article titled "Why do people earn what they earn?" (11/2/14), a *Boston Globe* reporter concluded that, "A cheerful, problem-solving server can be the difference between a customer heading straight to Yelp to vent and one who is so satisfied that she makes a follow-up reservation on the way out the door."

decades of research have consistently shown that higher employee engagement correlates very closely with higher individual and organizational performance. According to one study, "...when employees move from being disengaged to being highly engaged, their productivity improves 20 percentage points in performance levels." Another study found that highly engaged employees are twice as likely to be top performers.

At the organizational level, many other studies indicate that higher levels of engagement are associated with better performance on a wide range of critical metrics, including profitability, customer loyalty, productivity, employee turnover, safety, absenteeism, and quality. The specific findings vary, and the connection between employee engagement and performance is more (or less) direct for various metrics, but overall, I find data like these compelling:

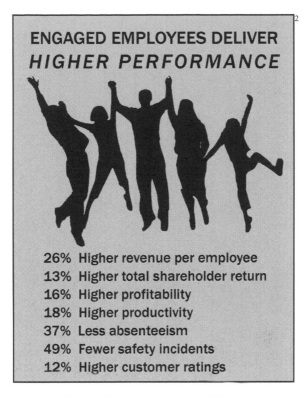

ENGAGED EMPLOYEES DELIVER
HIGHER PERFORMANCE

26% Higher revenue per employee
13% Higher total shareholder return
16% Higher profitability
18% Higher productivity
37% Less absenteeism
49% Fewer safety incidents
12% Higher customer ratings

The bottom line? If you want to build an organization that consistently delivers high levels of performance, your action plan should include building the kind of culture that stimulates high levels of employee engagement. Is that easy to do? No. Is it worth doing? What do you think?

---

2 The data included in this chart are taken from *The Impact of Employee Engagement on Performance*, InSync Surveys, LTD, 2012, an excellent review of engagement-related research. Available at http://www.insyncsurveys.com. au/media/92145/impact_of_employee_engagement performance.pdf

INTRODUCTION

CHAPTER 1

Is this Book For You?

THIS BOOK IS FOR YOU IF YOU LEAD, OR ASPIRE TO LEAD, AN organization of any size, for-profit or not-for- profit, early stage or mature—so long as you really and truly understand that *the organization's success, and therefore your own success, absolutely depends on the other people in the organization.* Whatever goals you need to achieve, you can't do it alone.

This book is for you if you believe that all work has dignity, that the people who do that work have dignity, and that for an organization to be successful over the long term, it must treat all of its people with dignity and respect.

This book is for you if too many people in your organization will do their job, but will also respond with "that's not my job" when something extra is needed. It's for you if you've figured out that you can't force people to be great or even to want to be great.

This book is for you if you're personally uncomfortable with leaders who always take the credit, who always step into the limelight—leaders who seem to suck all the air out of the room. It's for

> Much of this book is about creating high levels of engagement across an entire "enterprise." That said, the leaders with the most direct impact on engagement are the supervisors, department heads, and managers who work closely every day with relatively small groups of people to get stuff done. So even if you're a long way from the C-suite—at least for now—this book is for you too.

you if you know for sure that leadership is never about demeaning, bullying, or taking advantage of people.

Finally, this book is for you if your organization—whether it's a small department or a huge enterprise—is failing to achieve its key metrics. It's for you if you're committed to turning this situation around, not with a quick fix but with the kind of sustained effort it takes to create an organizational culture that really gets people excited about their work, the kind of high engagement organization where most people on most days bring their A-game to work.

WHAT'S THE BOOK'S MAIN POINT?

The book is built around a pretty straightforward argument:

1. *Organizations whose employees are highly engaged significantly outperform those where this is not the case.*
2. *As a leader you can't force your people to be highly engaged, but you can create an environment and culture that encourages them to become engaged.*
3. *The single most important thing an organization's leaders can do to promote engagement is to demonstrate that they care about their people.*

WHAT'S INCLUDED IN THE BOOK?

The book explores what engagement is all about, why it's important, and what key drivers tend to

Five Core Principles

promote it. It lays out a set of *five core principles* that can help your organization become an engaged enterprise—one where the great majority of people, day in and day out, make the extra effort necessary to achieve the best possible performance. To give you a better idea of what those principles look like when they're applied in the real world, the book also includes lots of stories—stories from my personal experience and that of other leaders who've built highly engaged organizations. In the final chapter I've also included some tools and exercises to help you develop an engagement plan for your own organization.

In the *Notes from the Field* chapters that appear at the end of each section, I've described in some detail key aspects of Cleveland Clinic's successful engagement initiative—an initiative designed to transform the culture and deliver higher levels of service excellence. The *Notes from the Field* idea is based on my experience as a fly fisherman. Whenever I

Notes from the Field

get out on the stream, I take notes on the weather and water conditions, what worked, what didn't, and so on. When I run into similar conditions on another day or another stream, those field notes are often a great guide to what I should do. I hope the field notes in this book will serve the same purpose for you as you work to turn your organization into an engaged enterprise, even if your organization is much smaller than Cleveland Clinic, even if it's far removed from healthcare.

WHERE DO THE IDEAS IN THE BOOK COME FROM?

The book draws on an extensive body of research and literature dealing with organizational change, employee engagement, leadership, and other topics related to what makes organizations successful.

Most of all this is a personal story, based on my more than 30 years of Human Resources experience in three different industries. That includes serving as the top HR executive at Cleveland Clinic, Blue Cross Blue Shield of Massachusetts, and the $4.5B Global Services Division of Digital-Compaq, as these three very different organizations transformed their cultures to achieve high levels of engagement and dramatically improved performance. In these roles I've had the good fortune to work with and learn from many outstanding individuals, including CEOs, GMs, and other senior executives; HR professionals; managers and employees; and thought leaders from the business, academic, and consulting sectors. This book incorporates the lessons I've learned from this experience and from these invaluable relationships.

I've written this book not because I have all the answers. No one does, and I *know* that I don't. I've written this book because my whole career has been about helping organizations to bring out the best in their people. That's why I chose a career in Human Resources. It's also the way I was trained to think by my earliest mentors, who believed passionately that getting the most out of its people was the only way for an organization to succeed.

You can't force people to connect emotionally with their work. The only way to get them to do that is to demonstrate that the organization and its leaders at every level respect them for who they are, what they think, what they do. As a leader, everything you do counts.

Treating your people with respect doesn't mean that tough decisions will never have to be made. It doesn't mean that benefits won't ever need to be reduced, that employees with skills that are no longer needed won't have to be let go, or that downsizing will never be required. It does mean that those decisions should never be made lightly. Every effort must be made to honestly communicate why they must be made and to mitigate their effects on the people most affected. It means that you should not treat your employees as a discretionary expense.

Treating people with respect doesn't mean that managers should tolerate or excuse poor performance. In fact, it is fundamentally *disrespectful* not to expect people to perform well. Treating people with respect *does* mean that the organization simply will not tolerate those who confuse strong leadership with not listening to others, never admitting mistakes, or being abusive.

There's nothing "soft" about any of this. This is about the hard work of building the kind of organization that can compete effectively in today's hyper-competitive, innovation-driven environment.

BE PREPARED FOR A BUMPY ROAD.

Assuming that your organization needs to change if it's going to achieve and sustain high levels of employee engagement and assuming that you see yourself playing a key role in driving that change, you should know that the odds of your being successful aren't great. In fact, according to Walter McFarland, Chairman of the Board of the American Society of Training and Development,

"…most organizational change efforts underperform, fail, or make things worse[3]."

You should also know that if you *are* successful, getting there will take longer than you'd like. Along the way you'll have some really tough days at the office.

Change is hard …

That's because organizations and the people in them seem to be hardwired to resist change. Even in the face of compelling evidence that an organization's current *modus operandi* isn't producing the desired results, there will almost certainly be fierce resistance to change. If that sounds like a definition of insanity—doing the same thing over and over again and expecting a different result—so be it.

On the other hand, change *is* possible. At Cleveland Clinic in 2008, a Gallup survey found that the ratio of engaged to actively disengaged employees was 2.5 to 1. According to Gallup's research a 4 to 1 ratio is considered "neutral," where engaged employees just counterbalance the negative

… but change is possible.

impact of their disengaged co-workers. In world class organizations the engaged/disengaged ratio is 9.6 to 1. So the Clinic was facing a pretty daunting challenge.

Five years later, after a concerted effort to transform itself into a "great place to work and grow," the Clinic had achieved sufficient organizational change to drive its engaged-disengaged ratio up to 10.2 to 1. What's equally noteworthy is that over the same five years, the Clinic's patient satisfaction performance rose in direct parallel to its engagement level.

So yes, positive, effective organizational change is possible—if you embrace the challenge—but don't think it will come quickly or easily.

---

3   http://blogs.hbr.org/2012/10/this-is-your-brain-on-organizational-change/

CHAPTER 2

THE POWER OF ONE ...
THE POWER OF YOU

EVERYTHING IN MY LIFE—THE SPECIAL EXPERIENCE OF GROWING up with an identical twin brother; the relationships with family members, teachers, coaches, colleagues, and mentors that have made me who I am; the lessons I've learned on the athletic field; the work I've done in my professional capacity; my involvement with some wonderful non-profit organizations; my religious beliefs—everything in my life has taught me that no one succeeds alone. We are definitely "all in this together."

I also believe that each of us has the power to help move the ball down the field. Each of us can make a difference. As Robert Kennedy once said, "Few of us have the greatness to bend history itself. But all of us have the opportunity to change a small portion of events." You are the CEO of the organization you lead, no matter how large or how small it is, and in that sense you have the power and the opportunity to make a difference. What you do—indeed, *everything* you do—counts.

Let me tell you the story of Kent Keith, one of the most interesting people I've ever met. Back in the 1960s, as a 19-year-old sophomore at Harvard, Kent wrote a manual for high school student government leaders. The booklet, which included a set of Paradoxical Commandments, was later published by the National

Association of Secondary School Principals, and some 30,000 copies were eventually distributed[4].

Kent went on to earn a doctorate and a law degree. He rose to become Director of Hawaii's Department of Planning and Economic Development, served in the Cabinet of the Governor of Hawaii, and held a number of other executive positions, including president of Chaminade University in Hawaii and CEO of the Greenleaf Center for Servant Leadership.

Well into his career, some 25 years after he had first written those Paradoxical Commandments, they reappeared in Kent's life, completely unexpectedly. The Honolulu Chief of Police called Kent to say that a speaker at a conference he'd attended had included them in his presentation, identifying Kent as their author. Then a librarian at Chaminade University found the Commandments on the internet, and later a visiting professor told Kent that she had used them for years in her graduate classes. And then a speaker at a meeting of Kent's Rotary Club, shortly after Mother Teresa had died, read the Commandments, which he had found in a book titled *Mother Teresa: A Simple Path*. It turned out that Mother Teresa had posted the Commandments in her children's home in Calcutta. In Kent's words, "...the Paradoxical Commandments had spread around the world, and after twenty-five years they began to come back to me in various ways and shapes."

THE PARADOXICAL COMMANDMENTS

People are illogical, unreasonable, and self-centered.
Love them anyway.

If you do good, people will accuse you of selfish, ulterior motives.
Do good anyway.

If you are successful, you will win false friends and true enemies.
Succeed anyway.

The good you do today will be forgotten tomorrow.
Do good anyway.

---

4   See Keith, K, *Anyway: The Paradoxical Commandments*. NY: Penguin Putnam, 2002.

Honesty and frankness make you vulnerable.
Be honest and frank anyway.

The biggest men and women with the biggest ideas can be shot down by the smallest men and women with the smallest minds.
Think big anyway.

People favor underdogs but follow only top dogs.
Fight for a few underdogs anyway.

What you spend years building may be destroyed overnight.
Build anyway.

People really need help, but may attack you if you do help them.
Help people anyway.

Give the world the best you have and you'll get kicked in the teeth.
Give the world the best you have anyway.

The Paradoxical Commandments speak to the intrinsic rewards of just doing the right thing—even though you might not be appreciated or rewarded, and might even be punished for doing so. As Kent says "If you can do things not for the world's applause, you are free. Free to do what you feel is right. Free to be the person who you really are and want to be."

Kent's story points to the fact that we can all make a difference, if we choose to act—and we can never be sure how much of an impact our actions will have. Even if you're not one of the senior leaders in **You can make a difference.** your organization, go ahead and apply some of the ideas to be found in these pages. You'll certainly make a difference in the lives of the people around you—and you never know, what you do may, like Kent Keith's Paradoxical Commandments, spread much further than you would ever have imagined.

Never underestimate the Power of One—the Power of You!

CHAPTER 3

WHY DON'T WE TREAT ENGAGEMENT LIKE ANY OTHER IMPORTANT STRATEGIC OBJECTIVE?

MOST ORGANIZATIONS ENGAGE IN SOME KIND OF STRATEGIC planning process. Objectives are defined, quantified, prioritized, and cascaded down from enterprise level to small units across the organization. Action plans to meet those objectives are drawn up at every level. Performance against those plans is measured and evaluated. As conditions change, goals and action plans are revised and refined. That's how you succeed, right?

And yet, in my experience, and from what I've gathered about other organizations, increased employee engagement is not always treated as a high priority strategic objective. That's despite the fact that most organizations and most leaders are quick to say that "our employees are our most important asset."

> Is increased employee engagement one of your organization's stated strategic objectives?
>
> If not, why not?

This is surprising when you consider that engagement correlates with such key metrics as revenue, profits, market share, customer retention and quality. Even if you didn't know about the research that demonstrates this correlation, wouldn't you think it was intuitively obvious that having a more highly engaged workforce would help an organization achieve many of its objectives?

Why isn't increased engagement always a high priority strategic objective? Why isn't it a key goal of your organization to generate that *"heightened intellectual and emotional connection ... that influences employees to apply additional discretionary effort to their work?"* Why isn't engagement one of those critical metrics tracked on the executive dashboard? Why isn't every leader, at every level, required to have an engagement plan for his or her unit?

> **Does your organization measure the ongoing efforts and results related to employee engagement?**

I don't get it. Do you? If your organization doesn't make engagement a priority, it will never become an engaged enterprise.

Now let's talk more specifically about what it takes to move the needle on employee engagement.

CHAPTER 4

THE FIVE PRINCIPLES

Building the Engaged Enterprise: 5 Core Principles

1. Real change starts with real dissatisfaction.
2. When a mission becomes personal, it becomes a cause.
3. If you don't care, they won't care.
4. Old habits die hard, so hardwire the change.
5. It's about building pyramids, not sand castles.

WE'LL BE DISCUSSING EACH OF THESE FIVE PRINCIPLES IN SOME detail later, but for now let me say just a few words about what they are and what they are not. These principles are lessons I've learned from my personal experience in organizations undergoing significant change, reinforced by what I've learned from the extensive literature on this topic. They are observations about what successful organizational change seems to involve, but they are not a set of rules that will absolutely guarantee successful change.

These principles are like the guardrails along the side of a highway. There is plenty of room within those guardrails for you and others to maneuver as circumstances dictate, but the guardrails define what in general is the safe route for you to follow. They can be very valuable in keeping you out of serious difficulty and helping you reach your destination.

These principles—and this book as a whole—are intended to be *descriptive* rather than *prescriptive*. They aren't intended to tell you exactly what to do in order to build an engaged enterprise, but rather, to describe what the process of building an engaged enterprise looks like in the real world. How you apply the principles and the examples presented throughout the book will depend on your particular situation. You have to choose which lane to travel in, when to hit the gas pedal and when to hit the brake, and how to navigate through the traffic and changing road conditions.

So let's get started on what I hope will be an exciting journey.

SECTION 1

REAL CHANGE
STARTS WITH REAL
DISSATISFACTION

CHAPTER 5

HARNESSING THE POWER
OF DISSATISFACTION

THE GREEK PHILOSOPHER HERACLITUS ONCE SAID, "NO MAN ever steps in the same river twice, for it's not the same river and he's not the same man." (As an angler, I'm especially fond of that quote.) We live in a world that is constantly changing all around us; to the point that you might say change is really the only constant in our lives.

And yet, when it comes to making a change in our lives, we find it incredibly hard to do. Health clubs are so busy right after New Year's, when so many of us resolve to get back in shape, that you can't even get on a machine—but things go right back to normal after a month or so, when the impulse to change (as opposed to the pounds) melts away.

There's no way around it: change is hard. It's hard for individuals, and in many ways it's even harder for organizations, with their hundreds and often thousands of individuals, each with his or her own tolerance of—and resistance to—any given change.

So here you are. You've concluded that your organization needs to change if it's going to build a highly engaged workforce. You know that you can't make that change happen by yourself: you're going to need buy-in from people all across the organization, especially the senior leadership team.

You also know that some of those **Change always encounters resistance.**

people will resist. Some will argue that no change is necessary; some will agree that change is needed, but just not the particular change you have in mind. (In that case, don't hold your breath waiting for them to come up with suggestions of their own.) And some will just adopt a passive resistance strategy, withholding their support and hoping that you'll give up and leave things as they are.

How do you overcome that resistance? You leverage the dissatisfaction that exists in your organization to build a strong business case for change.

DISSATISFACTION CREATES THE CLIMATE FOR CHANGE.

There's dissatisfaction in any organization, because organizations are just collections of people, and most people are dissatisfied with something at least some of the time. Under the right circumstances, that dissatisfaction can be a critical component in driving positive change. If you think about any significant change you've ever made in your personal or professional life, didn't it come about because you were deeply dissatisfied with something? You changed because you felt absolutely compelled to change.

The role of dissatisfaction in organizational change has been expressed in this formula: D x V x F > R. In order to overcome the inevitable **Resistance** to change in an organization, there has to be significant **Dissatisfaction** with the current situation, as well as a compelling **Vision** of something better and a set of practical **First Steps** to move the organization toward that desired future state. In other words, dissatisfaction creates the state of mind that enables change to occur.

Dissatisfaction at the more senior levels of leadership is especially crucial. Any significant organizational change, including change focused on increasing engagement, involves a whole array of decisions around policy, processes, priorities, and investments—and those decisions get made at the top of the house.

> Dissatisfaction at the top of the house.

To win support for change among your organization's senior leaders, you need to start by identifying and, if necessary, stimulating their dissatisfaction with key areas of organizational performance. Make the business case that one of the best ways to improve performance in those areas is to increase employee engagement. It's easier to make the case for metrics like productivity, customer satisfaction, quality, etc., but as we've already seen, it can be made for virtually any key metric. The point is, if you can connect those dots, you're on your way.

THE REALITY, OF COURSE, IS THAT YOU'RE NOT GOING TO GET EVERYONE'S SUPPORT.

The conventional wisdom is that no matter what proposal you make, one third of the people will readily agree, one third will disagree no matter what, and one third could go either way. Whether those specific numbers are correct, it's a safe bet that some of the leaders in your organization will be with you from the get-go. Like you, these people understand the connection between engagement and performance and already have a sense that your organization needs to do more to become an engaged enterprise.

Some members of the leadership team will disagree with you no matter how strong a business case you make. Some of these people just don't think engagement is, or should be, a major issue: "We pay people to do their job. If they're unhappy about something, they should either get over it or leave, but if they stay, they need to do their job, at the level of performance that's expected of them."

There are also the cynics and political infighters, the people who are more committed to their own success than the company's, the people who just don't want you to get a win, even if it's the best thing for the organization. They have their own agenda, and supporting you isn't part of it. Sometimes, supporting the mission of the organization isn't part of their agenda either.

The people you want to focus on are those who are dissatisfied with some areas of the organization's performance and are open to reasonable ideas for improvement, but who don't clearly see the connection to engagement. These people may be skeptical, but they're committed to the organization's mission. They're not cynical, but they need to be convinced that what you're proposing is not just another business fad, that it's realistic and doable, that it has a good chance of being successful. You need these people, because they ask tough questions and keep you honest. If you can make a strong case for change, they'll support you.

TAPPING INTO EMPLOYEE DISSATISFACTION.

For individual employees, dissatisfaction seems to be largely personal. "I can't stand my boss." "That's the second time I've been passed over for promotion." "How do they expect me to do my job if I can't even get the [fill in the blank] I need?" "My boss never says thank you, no matter what I do."

> What three words do you think best capture how your employees feel about your organization?
>
> What would you guess are the top three complaints your employees have about your organization?

If you listen closely and look for the commonalities, you'll find that your employees' complaints often point toward a few key aspects of your organizational culture. The way the organization's leaders behave, the kind of behaviors that are tolerated or actually rewarded, the opportunities—or lack of opportunities—for employees to advance: these are just a few of the ways your culture could be generating employee *dis*satisfaction.

Because employee dissatisfaction tends to focus on these more "personal" issues doesn't mean that the more performance-driven, enterprise-level issues don't matter to them. How well or poorly the organization succeeds in achieving its strategic goals could ultimately affect whether or not the employees actually have a jobs. As we'll discuss in a later section (*When a Mission Becomes Personal...*), the more the people in an organization come to define and understand its core mission in personal terms, the more highly engaged they are likely to be. Helping our employees make this connection is our job as leaders.

The problem is that whatever the nature of dissatisfaction at the employee level, in most organizations it tends to go unheard by the organization's leaders. Why? Because in most organizations, the employees believe, often rightly, that their leaders "don't want to hear about it." As a result, employee dissatisfaction all too often festers and promotes not engagement but *dis*engagement.

The first step to understanding what's causing dissatisfaction across your organization is to practice some *Management By Walking Around*. Eventually you'll probably want to invest in a survey or other more formal approach, but you'd be surprised how much you can learn by just being there and listening. Most of the time, the only question I have to ask to get the conversation rolling is, "What's keeping you up at night?"

The key is to stop thinking of dissatisfaction—whether at the executive level, the mid-management level, or the employee level—as something negative, and

> **Dissatisfaction is your friend.**

instead embrace it, understand its importance and its value, and then leverage it to create a powerful engine for positive change.

> What areas of organizational performance are causing the most dissatisfaction to your leadership team?
>
> Would increased employee engagement improve performance in those areas?

If you're trying to transform your organization and take your performance to new heights, dissatisfaction is your friend.

CHAPTER 6

Notes from the Field

In December of 2007, I joined Cleveland Clinic as its Chief Human Resources Officer. A large, complex enterprise, the Clinic at that time had some 40,000 employees. Its institutional footprint included the ever-expanding "main campus" in Cleveland; 10 community hospitals and numerous other patient care facilities throughout Ohio; a hospital in Florida; and an outpatient clinic in Toronto. Groundbreaking had taken place in 2007 for a new "brain center" in Las Vegas, and a plan was on the drawing boards for a new state-of-the-art hospital in Abu Dhabi.

The Clinic is one of the world's leading healthcare providers, drawing patients from over 100 countries every year. In the annual *US News & World Report* survey of US hospitals, the Clinic perennially ranks among the top four. In cardiac care, it has been ranked #1 every year since 1996.

In 2003, Dr. Delos "Toby" Cosgrove, then the Chair of the Clinic's cardiothoracic surgery department, had taken over as CEO. Under his leadership the Clinic had not only grown, but had also reorganized around more than 20 "Institutes," each of which brought together in one location all the specialties related to a particular set of medical issues—cardiovascular, oncology, pediatrics, etc. Buttressed by the aggressive use of new technology and efficient management practices, the Institutes were designed to enable more patient-centric care, prompting President Obama, during a 2009 visit, to comment that "Cleveland Clinic is simply a role model for some of the kind of changes [in healthcare] that we want to see."

Cleveland Clinic was definitely a high performance organization. Yet, as I was going through the interview process for the CHRO position, the CEO and some of the other senior leaders expressed a strong sense that despite the Clinic's success, some aspects of its culture needed to change.

> Even great organizations sometimes need to change.

Shortly after coming on board, I got a sense of this from a rather amusing incident at a quarterly staff meeting attended by most of the Clinic's physicians. Looking around the crowded auditorium, I spotted an empty seat near the back and asked the doctor sitting next to it if the seat was available. He said yes and as I settled in, I made some comment about there being "no assigned seats." He came right back, saying, "I'm surprised they don't have assigned seats, the way they treat us as children." Hmm, I thought, that's a data point.

The lights went down, the CEO launched into his remarks, and eventually he said, "Joe Patrnchak, our new Chief Human Resources Officer, is somewhere in the audience today, and I hope that either today or later you'll get a chance to welcome him to the Clinic." And at that point, my picture flashed up on the screen.

A few minutes later, the lights went up, and the doctor sitting next to me looked over and said, "Hi Joe. Welcome to the Clinic." Then he stood up and asked, "By the way, did I introduce myself?" When I said no, he said, "Good. Have a nice day." Before I could get a word out, he hurried off. In one way it was pretty funny. In another way, it wasn't. Incidentally, I never saw him again.

I picked up more signs of dissatisfaction over the next few weeks as I conducted my own informal walking-around survey, talking to people all across the organization. Some spoke openly, others were more careful in what they said and how they said it, but I definitely came away with my own strong sense that at least based on this small sample, a fair number of Clinic employees didn't feel valued by or closely connected to the organization.

Before I could plan, propose, and win support for any kind of major change initiative, however, I needed more than this anecdotal data.

CLEVELAND, WE HAVE A PROBLEM.

I reached out to the Gallup organization to conduct an enterprise-wide survey of employee engagement at the Clinic. As soon as news of the survey got out, HR began getting hundreds of e-mails from employees worried about confidentiality and the possibility of their being fired if they said anything negative! I had never before experienced that strong a reaction to just the *idea* of an employee survey—and that reaction alone told me something about what to expect from the survey itself.

Gallup conducted the survey in the spring of 2008, and the results made it absolutely clear that despite the Clinic's outstanding clinical results and worldwide reputation for excellence, we did have a serious engagement problem. When our overall engagement level was compared to other hospital systems, we ranked only in the 43rd percentile. As I've already indicated, our ratio of engaged to actively disengaged employees was only 2.5 to 1—a long way from the 4 to 1 ratio considered "neutral" and what looked like an impossibly long way from the 9.6 to 1 ratio Gallup describes as "world class."

Not surprisingly, these results provoked considerable dissatisfaction. To the people on the Clinic's leadership team—people who had risen to the top of their profession, who were accustomed to being, and being recognized as, best in class—the 43rd percentile in virtually anything was unacceptable.

Some of my colleagues chose to challenge the data, arguing that the engagement survey results were just wrong. One Institute Chair, whose engagement scores were among the lowest, took this tack, saying that "Everything

> Resistance to change takes many forms.

seems fine with my people," and pointing out that 500 employees had shown up for the Institute's recent barbecue lunch. "They wouldn't have shown up if they weren't engaged," he said. In response I suggested that showing up for a free lunch might not be the best evidence of high engagement.

Some other members of the executive team argued that even if the Clinic did have an engagement problem, that problem didn't seem to be having an impact on performance, so there was no need to get bent out of shape over it. To answer this objection, what was needed was significant dissatisfaction with some obviously important area of organizational performance that could clearly be tied to the Clinic's less than great level of engagement.

That's where the issue of the patient experience came in.

AND THEN THERE WAS HCAHPS.

For several years, the issue of the "patient experience" and patient satisfaction with that experience had been growing in importance in the healthcare space. This concern was partly driven by research indicating that the quality of the overall patient experience affects such important outcomes as recovery time and likelihood of a return to the hospital. It was also driven by the sense that consumerism has finally arrived in the healthcare market, that patients are increasingly demanding to be treated as customers, with corresponding expectations for high levels of service, and furthermore, that they will make "buying" decisions based on those expectations. In other words, people are increasingly making their own decisions about which hospital they will go to for care, and they are basing those decisions not just on whether a hospital can provide the necessary clinical care—in some sense, this is now just a minimum requirement—but also on the hospital's ability to provide them with a great service experience.

By 2008, the Clinic had taken a number of steps to improve its patient experience. The decision to reorganize into Institutes was at least in part driven by the desire to provide a more seamless, less confusing, and therefore "better" patient experience. The decision to appoint, in 2007, the Clinic's first Chief Patient Experience Officer was even more directly driven by this concern. At a different level, decisions about what kind of art to put on the walls and how to redesign the hospital gowns worn by patients were similarly driven.

But then, in the spring of 2008, the first HCAHPS results were published. HCAHPS—the Hospital Consumer Assessment of Healthcare Providers and Systems survey—is the first national, standardized, publicly reported survey of patients' perspectives of hospital care. The HCAHPS survey asks discharged patients 27 questions about their recent hospital stay. For each participating hospital, 10 HCAHPS measures are publicly reported by the government, dealing with everything from the responsiveness of physicians and nurses to how clean the rooms are and how quiet the halls are at night.

The Clinic's HCAHPS results in 2008 were not good. Our "overall" score was "average," and we were barely above average on the "would recommend" metric. In all the other, more specific metrics, our scores were below—often far below—the national average. In the words of the CEO, "People come to us, we save their lives, but they don't like us very much."

"People come to us, but they don't like us."

While some leaders argued that the whole focus on the patient experience was a potentially dangerous distraction from the real business of a hospital, which was actually solving medical problems, the fact remained that the HCAHPS results, widely publicized in the local media, struck at the Clinic's self-image. If those results did not improve in the future, they might well tarnish the Clinic's brand and ultimately have a negative effect on patient volume, which in turn had serious financial implications. This possibility was enhanced by the federal government's plan to run ads in local newspapers urging people to visit its "Hospital Compare" website to view HCAHPS scores. Finally, and perhaps most importantly, there was the fact that beginning in 2012, Medicare reimbursement rates would be tied to a hospital's HCAHPS results.

To say that the Clinic's HCAHPS results caused significant dissatisfaction within the senior leadership team is a considerable understatement. To most members of the senior leadership team, the connection between the Clinic's patient experience, as measured by the HCAHPS, and its engagement levels was immediately and intuitively obvious.

Without the dissatisfaction generated by the poor HCAHPS results, there might not have been enough support for a major engagement initiative. By itself, increased engagement might well have been seen as a "nice thing to do," not a "we have to do this." In today's world, "nice to do" rarely carries the day. But with those results, the stage was at least set to move forward.

As always, real change starts with real dissatisfaction. But that's just where it starts. Let's see what else it takes to build an engaged enterprise.

SECTION 2

WHEN A MISSION BECOMES PERSONAL, IT BECOMES A CAUSE

CHAPTER 7

Make It Personal

When was the last time you felt fully engaged in a project, whether at work or in some other aspect of your life? Do you remember how that felt? How success seemed so important—and failure so completely unacceptable—that you pushed yourself to do your very best? Do you remember how *personal* that project had become?

Members of the military, first responders, doctors and nurses—these people are likely to experience this deeply personal level of engagement when they are thrust into a life or death situation. But what about those of us whose work doesn't involve such obviously high stakes? Can we—should we—be this deeply engaged in our day-to-day activities? From an organizational perspective, can we create an institutional culture and a work environment that encourages our people to feel this way about their work?

Let's be clear: there's a huge difference between what most of us do every day and being in combat or running into a burning building or saving someone's life on an operating table. That said, in organizations like Disney and Southwest Airlines that are known for delivering a great customer experience, everyone's job, no matter how humble it may seem to be, is seen as important. Particularly in a service business, there's just no such thing as a "back office" job. You're either directly providing service to a customer, or you're providing service to someone who is. An organization that doesn't

> Every job touches the customer somehow.

understand this basic fact and act accordingly will never create a
true service culture—and without such a culture, the organization will never deliver truly world class service.

But even in a service business, saying that every job is important doesn't mean that every role is the same. In a hospital, for
example, there's no doubt that the doctors and nurses have the
most critical role to play in meeting the patients' clinical needs—
and that gives them a unique position within the organization.
But that doesn't mean that all the other people who work at the
hospital, and the jobs they do, are unimportant.

To the hungry patient in Room 4-110 who hasn't eaten all day
because of the tests she's gone through, the person who brings in
her dinner—and takes a few minutes to chat about what's on the
menu—may well be at that moment the most important person
in the hospital. To the patient in 8-222 who's on her way to a lab
for tests and is feeling nervous about what the results might be, the
transport person who takes her mind off her worries with a funny
story while pushing her wheelchair down the corridor is pretty
important. To the patient who's home from the hospital and has
questions about the bill that just arrived in the mail, the clerk in
accounting who takes her phone call certainly has an important
role to play in how that patient feels about the hospital.

The point is that everyone in an organization can make a difference. And they're far more likely to do what it takes if they really
feel that they and their work are important to the success of the
organization, if they feel that they have a personal stake in that
success. When people make that connection, the mission of the
organization becomes a personal cause.

What would it mean to your organization if your people felt
that way?

TAKE YOUR MISSION STATEMENT OFF THE WALL.

Most organizations of any size have a formal mission statement.
You can find it on their website, in the annual report, in various
locations around the workplace.

The mission statement is the organization's answer to the question, "Why are we here? Why do we exist?" It articulates a vision

of what the organization aspires to be and pledges itself to achieve, points the organization toward a higher purpose, and casts the everyday push and pull of the organization's activities in a brighter light. (That's why you don't see mission statements that say, "We're here to crush our competitors and make as much money as possible.")

Nike, for example, talks about bringing "inspiration and innovation to every athlete in the world," noting that "if you have a body, you're an athlete." Apple talks about "bringing the best personal computing experience to students, educators, creative professionals and consumers around the world." Google's says its mission is "to organize the world's information and make it universally accessible and useful."

> Millennials, who will make up nearly 50% of the US workforce by 2020, place an especially high value on work that "makes a difference in the world."
>
> How does your organization's mission help to attract and retain the best of this new generation?

But while people will certainly work to achieve a mission, they'll give everything they have for a cause. For your organization's mission statement to really inspire and engage your people—for it to become a personal cause—it has to become part of the everyday conversation, the everyday life, of the organization. It has to become part of your institutional belief system.

Peter Mercury, my boss at Digital Equipment Corporation, and one of the savviest executives I've ever worked with, used to say:

Tell me, and I'll forget.
Show me, and I'll remember.
Engage me, and I'll understand.

One way to engage your employees in understanding and personalizing the organization's core mission is to provide a setting in which they can periodically come together to think and talk about how their everyday work relates to the higher purpose expressed in the mission statement. It's a challenge to make that kind of time available and provide the kind of structure that produces meaningful conversation, but by doing it you're sending a clear message that the mission matters.

You can also use your institutional vocabulary to reinforce the connection between the organization's employees and its mission. At Cleveland Clinic, for example, employees are now referred to as caregivers, whether they're clinical staff who work directly with patients or they work in facilities, the kitchen, or in accounting. We'll talk in the upcoming *Notes from the Field* about what it took to make that change happen and what else was involved, but for the moment let me just say that it definitely helped connect our employees to our core mission and turn that mission into a personal cause that had a positive effect on our engagement level.

Steps like this won't mean much unless you and your fellow leaders demonstrate that the mission statement means something to *you*. As a leader, everything you do or say counts. The decisions you make, the actions you take, the behaviors you recognize and reward will ultimately determine whether your organization's mission statement comes to life or remains just empty words on your website.

For example, if your mission statement says that your organization is committed to providing customers with the highest level of service, but your managers actually discourage or prevent employees from doing what it takes to solve a customer's problem—then the result will be cynicism, not engagement.

If your mission statement talks about delivering top quality products, but employees who point out quality issues are ignored, stifled, or punished, then you might as well toss the mission statement out the window.

If your mission statement talks about integrity and honesty and respect, but people who regularly undercut their colleagues are tolerated and still get promoted, the result will again be cynicism, not engagement.

> **Food for Thought**
>
> Enron's mission statement was, "We treat others as we would like to be treated ourselves. We do not tolerate abusive or disrespectful treatment. Ruthlessness, callousness and arrogance don't belong here."

On the other hand, if employees who behave as if they really believe your mission statement are recognized and rewarded for that behavior, there's a much greater likelihood that your mission statement will become a cause that drives higher levels of engagement.

The point is that building an engaged enterprise takes much more than just setting aside time to discuss the corporate mission statement. It takes more than calling your employees "associates" or "partners." It takes more than a few new policies and programs aimed at getting a higher score on the next employee engagement survey.

Building an engaged enterprise is about building an enterprise that lives up to its higher purpose and, therefore, earns and *deserves the* full engagement of all its people.

Is your organization's mission clear and easy to understand?

What's your organization's promise?

Does it create emotion?

Do your people see themselves in your mission?

CHAPTER 8

LET YOUR PEOPLE SERVE

TODAY, BLUE CROSS BLUE SHIELD OF MASSACHUSETTS IS THE
largest health insurer in Massachusetts. It is consistently ranked
as one of the top private health plans in the country for clinical
performance and member satisfaction. It is also rated as one of the
Best Places to Work in Massachusetts.

But in the early 90s, the story was very different. In those days,
BCBSMA was on a downward spiral financially, to the point where
it was in receivership and in danger of losing its Blue Cross Blue
Shield accreditation. Its reputation was in tatters, and employee
morale was near rock bottom.

In 1992 Bill Van Faasen stepped in as BCBSMA's new CEO.
With every move monitored by a state-appointed regulator, he and
his team set out to develop a successful turnaround strategy, but
nothing they tried made enough of an impact. Then one day, while
sitting on a plane, Van Faasen had one of those moments of sud-
den clarity. Looking through the results of customer focus groups,
he realized that the one thing customers valued most was service.
Yet, improving service quality barely figured into any of the turnaround strategies that he and his team had been pursuing.

As soon as he got back to Boston, he pulled his team together
to see where this insight might lead. Ultimately it led to the decision to make service the organization's #1 priority, to put service
at the core of the growth strategy. A new "concierge" service was
introduced, with a promise to customers that when they called
BCBSMA their question would be answered, their problem would

be solved, and their issue would be resolved—period. To deliver on that promise, the people on the other end of those calls, BCB-SMA's customer service representatives, were re-trained and given more autonomy. Equally important, their key performance metric shifted from how fast they handled an incoming call to how successfully they resolved the caller's issue.

In meetings held all across the organization, leaders communicated the same message to the employees, who, by the way, were now referred to as "associates":

> *There's no back office here. No matter what our job is, we all have a crucial role to play in serving our members. The only way we will succeed is by "putting members first, so let's make service the core of our growth strategy"*

It took time, but the message took hold. Service quality improved, and the business began to recover. By the time I joined BCBSMA as its Chief Human Resources Officer in 2002, the company was financially sound again, and its reputation, like its finances, had completely turned around. You could feel the passion for great service all across the enterprise, in every function and at every level.

I remember sitting in on some of the incoming calls from members and being surprised at how many of them really should have been—from a purely cost-effective viewpoint--directed somewhere else. There were questions about bills that only the hospital could answer, calls about medical appointments that only the doctor's office could answer. Instead of telling the member to call the hospital or the doctor's office, the BCBSMA customer service rep took care of the problem. They made those calls themselves, they did the homework, they found the answer, and they got back promptly to the member.

Is this the most cost-efficient way to run a call center? Not if you measure cost efficiency just in terms of handling time. But if you look at the broader picture and think in terms

> How does customer service fit into your organization's growth strategy?
>
> What might be getting in the way of your delivering great customer service?

of customer satisfaction and loyalty, you might come to a very different conclusion.

Before joining BCBSMA, I had been at Digital Equipment Corporation, which then became part of Compaq Computer Company and then Hewlett Packard. As head of HR for Global Services, I worked with the Harvard Business School team that developed the idea of a Service Profit Chain. Drawing on their study of many leading service-based companies, they demonstrated the links between employee satisfaction, value to the customer, customer satisfaction and loyalty, and finally, profitability and growth.

One of their most important findings was that employee satisfaction in service businesses hinges on the employee's having the "ability and authority to achieve results for customers." Another key point is the importance of transforming *satisfied* customers into *loyal* customers. Loyal customers feel an emotional connection to the business. They're the repeat customers. They refer others to the company. They'll even pay more for the company's services.

> Have you ever led a group of volunteers?
>
> What lessons did you learn that you could use in your current role?

When I got to BCBSMA, it was clear that its leaders had connected these same dots. They had applied the concepts of the Service Profit Chain[5], even though they hadn't used that language. They had empowered their "associates" to deliver great service. By doing so, they had created not only satisfied, but also loyal, customers. That had turned the business trajectory from decline to growth, from failure to success.

What might happen if your organization made the same connection between engaged empowered employees and great customer service? If you connected those dots, how much more successful could you become?

---

5   See Heskett, J; Jones, T; Loveman, G; Sasser, W; Schlesinger, L. "Putting the Service Profit Chain to Work." *Harvard Business Review*, March 1994. Also, *The Service Profit Chain*, by the same authors; New York: The Free Press; 1997.

CHAPTER 9

WHAT IF WE TREATED OUR
EMPLOYEES LIKE VOLUNTEERS?

OVER THE YEARS I'VE HAD THE PRIVILEGE AND PLEASURE OF being involved with a number of non-profit organizations. As these organizations evolved, they brought on board a small number of paid staff, but they also continued to depend on dedicated volunteers to accomplish their mission. How does that work? What inspires those volunteers to give up their time? How does the organization keep them coming back? How does a leader's behavior change when the people he's leading can just walk away?

In my experience, non-profits go to great lengths to tell a compelling story—a story that gives volunteers and potential volunteers a gut sense of what the organization really means to the people it serves. They tell stories about their volunteers and how those volunteers contribute to the organization's mission. They celebrate the volunteers as heroes.

Organizations that depend on volunteers also manage with a light touch—not by telling the volunteers what to do but by explaining what needs to be done and how to do it. They try as much as possible to play to their volunteers' strengths, to give them a choice of how to participate, and they do what they can to make the work interesting and fun. And perhaps most of all, they thank their volunteers often and in different ways. When they say thank you, they really mean it. They understand that without those volunteers the organization could not succeed.

Of course, most people go to their day job because they get paid to do that job, and the money they earn is what houses, clothes, and feeds them and their families. But money alone can't produce that *"heightened emotional and intellectual connection that an employee has for his/her job, organization, manager, or co-workers that, in turn, influences him/her to apply additional discretionary effort to his/her work."*

In other words, money can't buy engagement. Conversely, non-profits have proven that engagement can be stimulated without money. So what if we treated our employees as volunteers? What if we treated them as if they could just walk away—which is true for those whose skills are most in demand? How would we change as leaders, how would our organization change, how would our people respond—and what results could we achieve?

CHAPTER 10

NOTES FROM THE FIELD

LIKE EVERY HOSPITAL, CLEVELAND CLINIC'S CORE MISSION—AS implied by its "Patients First" promise—is to provide the best possible care to its patients. Anyone who has ever worked at the Clinic would agree that this is a worthwhile mission. When Gallup first surveyed the Clinic's employees in 2008, this item on the survey—*the organization's mission makes me feel my job is important*—received a mean score of 3.8 on a 5-point scale. Not bad, but surprising for people working in a world class hospital, and hardly an indication that the Clinic's employees on the whole felt closely connected to its mission, much less that the mission had become a personal cause.

MAKING IT PERSONAL.
Cleveland Clinic's core mission has always been about caring for patients. But in today's increasingly consumer-driven healthcare market, providing the best possible care means more than just dealing with the patient's symptoms. While the number one priority is still to deliver outstanding clinical outcomes, in today's world patient care also means providing a total "experience" that meets an array of emotional, social, cultural, environmental, and clinical needs. (Remember that HCHAPS survey we discussed earlier?)

That more expansive definition of the Clinic's mission means that everyone who works there can and should be seen as having a role to play in patient care. Yet, not that long ago the Clinic's

institutional vocabulary actually communicated the opposite message, by dividing employees into "professional staff" and "non-professional staff."

How could anyone feel connected to the organization's mission when they were told that they were "non-professional?"

In the fall of 2008, a group of senior leaders, myself included,
met to discuss how to convey the message that everyone at the
Clinic touches the patient experi-
ence in some way. Eventually, the
phrase "We are all caregivers" sur-
faced in our discussion. Of all the ideas we considered, that phrase
resonated the most.

We are all caregivers.

But when we proposed a full-scale "We are all caregivers" initiative to the entire executive team, the response was decidedly
mixed, and the discussion was certainly what you might call "spirited." On the one hand, with the HCHAPS survey much in mind,
there was general agreement that all employees played a role in the
patient experience. For many of our physician-executives, the "we
are all caregivers" idea fit perfectly with the basic fact that medicine
was a team activity. As one Institute leader put it, "Put a great doctor in an average hospital and he'll get average results. Put an average doctor in a great hospital and they'll become a great doctor."

On the other hand, as at least some people expressed and to
quote one physician-executive, "I don't mean any disrespect to anyone, but the fact is doctors and nurses are the only caregivers here."
To these folks, the notion that someone working in the accounting
office or collecting parking fees in the garage could be considered a
caregiver was one of those "feel good" ideas that no one would take
seriously, because HCHAPS or no HCHAPS, it didn't deserve to
be taken seriously. Worse yet, a campaign based on this idea might
actually have the negative result of insulting and thereby *dis*-engag-
ing the doctors and nurses who really were caregivers.

In the end, though, with the support of the CEO, the idea
carried the day. In the coming months, "employee" was changed
to "caregiver" on all communications materials, from ID badges
to the Clinic website. The idea appeared in short video clips that
appeared on media displays in all facilities. The CEO, Chief Patient
Experience Officer, Chief Human Resources Officer, and other top

leaders wove the "we are all caregivers" theme into presentations to diverse Clinic audiences. Other programs that we'll be discussing later in these pages reinforced the idea in a variety of ways—and over time it became ingrained in the Clinic's institutional vocabulary, to the point where the 2010 Annual Report was titled *We Are All Caregivers*.

I'm convinced that the reason this simple change in language caught on the way it did is that it helped to personalize the organization's core mission. I'm also convinced that while this kind of language change isn't enough by itself to drive significant organizational change it can definitely contribute to the process. As one psychologist commented in the *Wall Street Journal*, "…it turns out that if you change how people talk, that changes how they think." And if you change how people think, you're on your way to changing how they behave.

> How does your institutional vocabulary encourage—or discourage—engagement?

CONNECTING THE DOTS.

There's a difference between believing something and internalizing it to the point where it changes your behavior. I may believe that working out regularly and getting more sleep would be good for me, but internalizing that belief to the point where I actually show up at the gym three days a week and hit the sack an hour earlier— that's a different thing entirely.

As the "We are all caregivers" campaign unfolded, it became clear that while some people still weren't buying the idea, it did resonate with a great many of our employees. The question then became how to build on the idea—how to take it from a change in language to a change in how the organization and all of us who worked there behaved on a day-to-day basis?

At least part of the answer was the "Cleveland Clinic Experience" program, which brought Clinic caregivers together in groups of 8 to 10, drawn from different functions and different levels of the organization, for a 3-hour discussion of the Clinic's mission and values.

> The Cleveland Clinic Experience

This was our organization "reset." A trained volunteer facilitator guided each group, helping to connect the dots between each person's job and the patient experience. Over a 6 month period, everyone at the Clinic participated in the program, with some 50 to 60 groups meeting on the same day—the first time that physicians had taken part in a learning activity with staff from all functions.

As with the "We are all caregivers" campaign, it wasn't easy to get buy-in from the senior leadership team, especially the physician-executives who made up the great majority of its members. Some argued that taking so many people off line would create a logistical and operational nightmare: "This is a complete waste of time. It's taking people away from what they really should be doing." Others simply said, "I'm too busy to take part in this kind of thing."

> Does your organization bring people together to discuss its mission?
>
> If not, why not?
>
> If so, do these activities produce the results you want?

The Chief Patient Experience Officer, himself a physician, played a key role in getting us over this hurdle by piloting the program with several hundred doctors working in his specialty area. When he brought their overwhelmingly positive responses back to the executive team some of the resistance dissipated.

Even so, after a series of discussions spread over more than eight months, it still looked as if the executive team would support the program for non-physicians, but would not support making participation mandatory for the docs. I have to admit that by this time, I was more than a little frustrated, to the point where I finally said, "Look, if we make the program voluntary for physicians but mandatory for everyone else, we're just reinforcing the idea that this is a two-tier organization, that physicians are a special class, entitled to be treated differently from everybody else. It seems to me that that's exactly the opposite of the message we're trying to communicate, and rather than do that, we'd be better off just not running the program at all."

That argument, combined with the positive responses to the Chief Patient Experience Officer's pilot program and the support of the CEO, seemed to produce a tipping point. However grudgingly in some cases, the senior leadership team finally got behind the program, including making participation mandatory for everyone. We were finally on our way!

The Cleveland Clinic Experience Program was built around a "learning map" that highlighted all the touch points a patient or family member has with Clinic staff, from the moment they first check in to the moment they leave at the end of their stay. The map provided a powerful visual stimulus that helped caregivers from across the hospital to see and to talk to one another about how their work related to the core mission of caring for patients.

Mapping the touchpoints.

The program also introduced a set of caregiver skills that reflected and would reinforce the Clinic's core values. Using the acronym HEART, this set of skills include how to listen closely and really *hear* the other person, *empathize* with the other person's situation, *apologize* when something has gone wrong, *respond* appropriately and with respect to the other person's concerns, and finally to say *thank you* and really mean it. All of the Clinic's line managers have been trained in how to build these skills into the everyday work of their units.

To implement the Cleveland Clinic Experience Program, over 300 staff members from all across the enterprise volunteered and were trained to lead discussion groups. One of the facilitators was a member of our environmental services staff who was a painter. He affectionately became known as "Jim the Painter." Jim led 25 of the CCE sessions. Commenting on his experience, he joked that "Those groups are the only time I get to put on a tie and talk to the doctors." But more seriously, he also commented that, "…it [the experience] changed my life. But what's even more important is that from the feedback I got, I helped change other people's lives as well."

I watched a number of Jim's sessions. It seemed clear that at first some of the participants—which included doctors, nurses, managers, and executives—were put off by the fact that he was the designated leader. You could see it on their faces: "This guy is the leader…a guy who normally would be painting walls around main campus?" And to be fair, Jim wasn't especially polished or articulate. On the other hand, his sincerity and commitment came through loud and clear, and before long, his groups were humming along. Later, when we collected evaluations, Jim always earned the highest possible ratings.

The question is whether programs like the "We are all care-givers campaign" and the Cleveland Clinic Experience training make a difference. Do they help to establish a personal connection between employees and the organization's core mission? Do they help to move the needle on engagement? At Cleveland Clinic, the answer was definitely yes.

MOVING THE NEEDLE.

One indication that these programs had an impact comes from the Gallup surveys, which over time showed a dramatic improvement in how employees responded to "the organization's mission makes me feel my job is important." The Gallup survey score for that item rose from 3.8 in 2008 to 4.23 in 2013, statistically speaking a very significant increase.

And then there's the anecdotal evidence. There's the financial analyst who commented: "… even though the finance group has no direct patient contact, information we provide can still affect the experience and outcomes of our patients." And this from a member of the media group: "Even though we are in a nonclin-ical field, we strongly believe we are tied to the Cleveland Clinic experience..."

There are also the comments from patients, including those from a man whose wife received a life-saving lung transplant at the Clinic in 2011. In discussing their experience at the Clinic, he commented that, "Doctors, nurses, housekeepers…people just seemed to care. There was a heart-to-heart connection, more so than just a clinical connection. On people's name tags, I noticed the phrase 'caregiver.' That phrase spoke to me. This was not just a slogan. This was something this entire staff believed in."

That's what can happen when a mission becomes a cause, when people start to believe that what they do makes a difference, and when they start bringing more of themselves to work every day.

So ask yourself this: how much more successful would your organization be if your people felt—and acted—that way?

SECTION 3

IF YOU DON'T CARE,
THEY WON'T CARE

CHAPTER 11

GREAT LEADERS ARE CARING LEADERS

IT DOESN'T TAKE A GENIUS TO FIGURE OUT THAT MOST PEOPLE will have real trouble feeling emotionally connected to an organization that doesn't give a hoot about them. So it's not surprising that the research on employee engagement has consistently found that one of the key factors in whether or not employees become highly engaged is whether or not they feel that their leaders care about them.

In my experience, most senior leaders *do* care. That's not to say that I haven't encountered my share of self-centered, arrogant executives who couldn't care less about anyone other them themselves. Those people are out there. You probably know a few yourself.

> Have your leaders made any decisions recently that might suggest to employees that the organization doesn't care about them?

But most of the people who end up in leadership roles are *not* self-centered or arrogant or uncaring. And yet, they—we—all too often make decisions and take actions that come across that way to our employees. Why is that?

One reason is that when we're in decision-making mode, and especially when the decision we have to make is a tough one, we often fail to include all of our stakeholders, including our employees, in our thought process. Peter Mercury, my boss at Digital, used to say that before making an important decision, he imagined himself explaining that decision to a conference room filled with a thousand employees and managers. In Peter's words, "If I can't explain the decision in a way that makes sense to those people—whether they like the decision or not is another question—then maybe I need to rethink it."

I also think that sometimes we regard our employees not so much as people but as just another resource—albeit a *human resource*. Resources are not something you care about. Resources are something you manage, optimize, utilize, etc.

And sometimes we're just tone deaf. We aren't sensitive to how our actions will be perceived. Part of the reason for that is that even though we may actually care about our employees, on a day-to-day basis we live in a different world. As senior leaders, we have far more power, we make a lot more money, and in many other ways we're treated as if we're special. In many organizations, we're the ones with the private parking spaces, offices on mahogany row, executive dining rooms, access to the company's luxury box at the ball park, first-class tickets and first-class hotels when we travel, not to mention the much better deal we get if we're "separated" from the company.

> Can you think of some "perks" that leaders in your organization have that other employees don't have?

You might think this "two-tier" treatment would prevent people from developing a positive emotional connection to the organization they work in. And in fact, it seems clear that Americans are increasingly unhappy about the wide gap in this country between the very wealthy and everyone else. It also seems apparent that this unhappiness extends to the compensation gap between CEOs and other top executives and the average worker. In *The Undeserving Rich: American Beliefs about Inequality, Opportunity, and Redistribution*, published in 2013, sociologist Leslie McCall analyzed research going back over 25 years. The result: clear evidence that Americans feel the income gap is too large and that "Americans... object to overpaying executives and underpaying workers."

That said, I'm not sure it means that employees in a given organization necessarily resent the difference in compensation and other perks received by their executives—*as long as this gap is not flaunted and the employees feel that they themselves are being treated fairly.*

What do I mean by flaunted? At one extreme, there's the case of the former CEO of TYCO, a $17B+ international conglomerate. You may remember the much publicized trial in 2005, in which he was convicted of receiving over $80M in unauthorized bonuses. His employees probably didn't know about the bonuses, at least until his trial, so you can't call that flaunting (although "unethical," "greedy and arrogant" certainly apply). But his employees certainly did know about the $2M birthday party he threw for his wife on the island of Sardinia, partly paid for by the company. Among other little touches, the multi-day extravaganza included a live Jimmy Buffett concert and an ice sculpture of Michelangelo's David that apparently squirted vodka from David's... Well, you get the point. That's flaunting.

But it doesn't take anywhere near that level of excess to damage the emotional connection between an organization and its employees. What about paying your leadership team big bonuses while not approving even modest increases for the rest of the workforce? What about increasing the employee contribution to their health insurance plan while spending millions on art for the new executive office suite? What about....?

> **Food for Thought**
>
> In a NY Times article (July 27, 2014), two Canadian psychologists wrote: "Can people in high positions of power easily empathize with those beneath them? Psychological research suggests the answer is no."
>
> The authors' own research looked at how the brain actually responds to feelings of power and found that "Power, it appears, changes how the brain itself responds to others."

All it takes for things to go south is for us as leaders to start taking the special treatment we enjoy as our due and for us to feel entitled to that treatment—instead of viewing it, and our role as leaders, as a privilege. When that happens, it's easy to start acting in ways that make us look an awful lot like those self-centered, arrogant, uncaring "takers" we don't ever want to be.

Let me turn back to the Cleveland Clinic Experience Program, which was discussed in the last chapter. The program was intended to strengthen the "we are all caregivers" concept, and the Clinic's executive team agreed that this was an important goal—so important that 500 caregivers at a time were taken "off line" to participate in the program. On the other hand, many members of the executive team seemed blind to the fact that allowing physicians *not* to participate would send a message to everyone else that said very clearly, "the docs are special and the rest of us are not." That's a far cry from the message the TYCO CEO's behavior sent, but it's one click away from "this organization cares about the physicians more than it cares about the rest of us," which could in turn very easily become "this organization doesn't care about me."

When I look back on this issue, I'm amazed at how hard it was to overcome resistance to this program. Seriously. Did participation in a three-hour Cleveland Clinic Experience meeting inconvenience our physicians? I'm sure it did. Did the physicians think that meeting with facilities workers, kitchen workers, and other "non-professional" staff was a waste of their time? I'm sure many of them did feel that way. But I'm also sure that not having the physicians participate would have turned "we are all caregivers" into empty words and significantly impaired the effort to turn the Clinic into an engaged enterprise. So this was an argument worth having.

In the end it always comes back to this: if you want your employees to care about your organization, you have to show them that the organization cares about them. And when I say "you," I'm not speaking in the abstract.

I'm talking about YOU.

IF NOT YOU, WHO?

If you've taken on the mission of transforming your organization into a truly engaged enterprise, you've also committed yourself to building an organization that really does care about its employees. That means that on many occasions you'll have to step up and be the one who represents your employees to your colleagues on the leadership team. You'll have to push your colleagues to support programs and policies that meet your employees' needs. You'll have to remind your colleagues of how a caring leadership connects to high levels of engagement and how that connects to high

Dare to care...

levels of performance. And sometimes you'll have to fight to keep your leadership team from making the wrong decisions—the kind that send a "we don't care" message. You'll have to dare to care.

This role can be frustrating and stressful. It will cause you more than a few sleepless nights. It can make you unpopular with your colleagues. It can even put your job at risk. Which reminds me of a wonderful book I read recently, called *The Unforgiving Minute*. It was written by Craig Mullaney, a West Point graduate who served as a platoon leader in Afghanistan. At one point, in the middle of an exhausting training exercise, one of his Ranger instructors says: "You are here for one reason. You are here for the troops you are going to lead. I don't care if you're tired, hurt, or lonely. This is for them. This isn't about you."

Leadership is a privilege, and with that privilege comes a tremendous responsibility, not only to make the correct strategic decisions and deliver the necessary financial results, but also to ensure the well-being of the people we lead. Doing all of this is not easy, and we should constantly be evaluating ourselves and asking if we're up to that responsibility. If we're not, we should step down.

SPEAKING TRUTH TO POWER.
In the interest of transparency, I should start this story by telling you that the main character, let's call her "Martha," is someone I've known and admired for many years. A few years ago, Martha was serving as the Chief Human Resources Officer for a faith-based, regional healthcare system with some 12,000 employees. She'd been in the job for about three years; her CEO had been there two.

The story begins in late winter when two female employees came to Martha's office, independently of one another, to report that the CEO had behaved inappropriately toward them. One of the women also reported that she knew two other employees who had had similar experiences with the CEO.

As required by law, Martha initiated an investigation, first involving two members of her HR team, then the parent organization's General Counsel, and finally an outside attorney. Ultimately, on the basis of the investigation and the organization's stated policy and previous actions in other cases, she recommended to the parent organization that the CEO be terminated.

When the head of the parent organization decided to issue a reprimand instead, Martha pushed back, arguing that the CEO should be held to the same standard as any other employee and that not doing so would send a very negative message to the employees. In a letter to the CEO and the Board, she said: "I cannot stand aside or participate in an effort to protect the institution and its powerful leader as priority over compassion for those injured by shameful and inexcusable conduct."

Not surprisingly, the incident made its way into the press. When the story broke, 10 more women came forward to report similar incidents with the CEO. Within a week, the parent organization reconsidered the decision to issue a reprimand. The CEO was offered the opportunity to resign, and he did so.

You may never face a situation as serious as this one. But I'm absolutely sure that you will face many situations where you'll know that your organization is heading down the wrong path. You'll know that a decision that's about to be made will tell your employees that their leaders don't care about them. In those moments—those defining moments when you'll be tempted to just keep your head down—I hope you'll decide not to do so. I hope you'll decide to follow Martha's example. She did what she knew was right, even while putting herself at risk.

> What "defining moments" have you faced?
>
> Are you ok with the way you responded?

If, in those defining moments, you do what's right, you won't always be successful. You won't win every argument. But you'll win some, and you'll be respected for having the courage to do the right thing without being told.

The decisions you make in those defining moments ultimately form the core of how others perceive you as a leader. This unique *leadership identity* precedes you into roles, relationships, and even important meetings. It affects what people expect from you, how they deal with you, and how they talk to others about you.

For better or for worse, your leadership identity walks into the room before you do. What do you want it to say about you?

CHAPTER 12

GREAT LEADERS PUT OTHERS FIRST

IN THE LAST CHAPTER WE FOCUSED ON THE UNIQUE ROLE SENIOR
leaders play in creating an organization that cares about its people
and elicits high levels of engagement. Now let's broaden the discussion to include all leaders, from the supervisor level right on up to
the C-suite. Leaders at every level play a crucial role in building an
engaged enterprise. In fact, the direct one-to-one relationship
between a line manager and an employee may well be the most
powerful single determinant of that employee's engagement level.
To quote from just one research study:

> *Employees [in the study] said that it is the personal relationship with
> their immediate supervisor that is the key [to their engagement].
> The attitude and actions of the immediate supervisor can enhance
> employee engagement or can create an atmosphere where an employee
> becomes disengaged.*[6]

How do you cre-
ate a caring mindset
in leaders at every
level of your organi-
zation, even if that
includes hundreds
or even thousands of

Food for Thought

In his best-selling *Good to Great,*
Jim Collins discussed the "Level 5
leader" as being modest, humble,
"willing to subjugate their own needs
to something larger and more lasting
than themselves," and attendant to
"people first, strategy second."

---

6   *What Drives Employee Engagement and Why It Matters, Dale Carnegie Train-
    ing and MSW Research,* 2010. Available at: http://www.dalecarnegie.com/
    assets/1/7/driveengagement_101612_wp.pdf.

supervisors and managers? Thousands of books have been written on the subject of leadership development, and many of those books include the idea that effective leaders care about the people around them. My guess is that you have some of those books on your bookshelf right now.

But of all the leadership concepts I've been exposed to, the one that has made the most lasting impression on me is Robert Greenleaf's idea of the Servant-leader. I'm so convinced of the importance of Greenleaf's ideas that for several years I've served on the Board of the Greenleaf Center for Servant Leadership. The Center, founded by Greenleaf in 1964, is dedicated to advancing the "awareness, understanding, and practice of servant-leadership by individuals and organizations."

WHAT IS A SERVANT-LEADER?

In his 1970 essay, *The Servant as Leader*, Greenleaf argued that what distinguishes servant-leaders is "the care taken [by the servant-leader] to make sure that other people's highest priority needs are being served[7]."

The servant-leader puts others first. Larry Spears, a past CEO of the Greenleaf Center and the author of hundreds of articles and books on servant-leadership, has identified 10 characteristics of a servant-leader: *listening, empathy, healing, awareness, persuasion, conceptualization, foresight, stewardship, commitment to the growth of people, and building community.*

You may not be familiar with the concept of servant-leadership, and some of its language may seem a bit unusual or even strange—"healing," for example, is not all that common a term in the literature of business—but most of Spears' characteristics are widely accepted, at least in theory, as being important to effective leadership. Who would argue that a leader should *not* be a good listener or not be able to empathize with others? Who would dispute the importance of a leader's being persuasive or being committed to the growth of the people in his or her organization?

---

7   Greenleaf, RK. *The Servant as Leader*. Westfield, IN: Greenleaf Center for Servant Leadership; 2008.

The problem is that all too often we don't actually behave in accordance with these ideas. I'm pretty certain, for example, that if I had asked the leaders at Cleveland Clinic back in 2008 whether or not "listening" and "empathy" were important leadership characteristics they would have overwhelmingly said, Yes. Yet, on that year's Gallup survey, our employees gave the organization only a 3.4 on a 5-point scale on the "My opinions count" item. That was the third lowest rating of the 12 items on the survey.

Similarly, I'm sure that the Clinic's leaders would have said that they were committed to the professional and personal growth of the people in the organization. Yet on that 2008 Gallup survey, "There is someone at work who encourages my development" received only a 3.7 rating, the fourth lowest score of the 12 items on the survey.

As for persuasion, as Spears notes in his discussion of this issue: "The servant-leader seeks to convince others, rather than coerce compliance. " As with other characteristics of servant-leadership, I suspect that most leaders at Cleveland Clinic and elsewhere think of themselves as generally relying more on persuasion than coercion. And yet how often do we as leaders forego persuasion and fall back on our "position power"? How often do we resort to command and control rather than look for ways to share power with those around us?

And by the way, applying the principles of servant-leadership doesn't mean that the organization *never* operates in a traditional command and control manner. In the military you're taught to follow orders or people can die. I'm sure when a surgeon, in the operating room needs something, they need it. As I mentioned I played 4 years of Big Ten football at Northwestern and when it was 3rd and short and the coach called the play we didn't do consensus management in the huddle. But when you're trying to create an engaged enterprise, where people are emotionally and intellectually connected and give you their discretionary effort, constant command and control just doesn't translate all that well.

DOES SERVANT-LEADERSHIP REALLY WORK?

The chances are that your organization already has some servant-leaders of its own, whether or not they or anyone else would use that terminology to describe how they operate. On the other hand, since you're reading this book, my guess is that, on the whole, you wouldn't describe your organization's leadership style as anything close to servant-leadership. Like most organizations, yours probably adheres to some form of the traditional, top-down, command and control leadership model. Maybe that's not so surprising, considering that most of us operate in a hyper-competitive environment where delivering results is Goal #1, and nothing else comes close.

So the question is, does servant-leadership (with or without the label) deliver results—and do it better than other leadership models? I think the answer is, Yes.

One of the best discussions of servant-leadership that I've ever seen is "The Essentials of Servant-Leadership: Principles in Practice," by Anne McGee-Cooper, Duane Trammel, and Matthew Kosec[8]. This article is so compelling that you should go online today and read every word. Your ideas about leadership may never be quite the same afterwards.

The article takes an in-depth look at how servant-leadership actually works, including mini-case studies of TD Industries and Southwest Airlines, both well known for their embrace of servant-leadership principles.

TD Industries is one of the country's largest mechanical construction companies, with annual revenues in excess of $400M. The company is both highly profitable and perennially listed by *Fortune* as one of the country's 100 Best Places to Work. At TD, everyone, including the executives, operates on a first-name basis; everyone in the corporate offices, including C-level executives, sits in an open cubicle. One hundred percent of the company's stock is owned by the 1800 or so employee/partners. As for performance, over the 20 years from 1992 to 2012 the value of that stock increased by 641%, compared to the S&P's 385%.

---

8   McGee-Cooper, A, Trammel, D, and Kosec, M. *The Essentials of Servant-leadership: Principles in Practice, 2013*. Available at: http://amca.com/amca/wp-content/uploads/The-Essentials-of-Servant-Leadership-Final.pdf.

Has servant-leadership been critical to TD's success? The company's website says: "At TD, Servant-Leadership is a way of life that deeply enhances our culture and our business." In the McGee-Cooper article, former CEO and current Board Chair Jack Lowe (also a former member of the Greenleaf Center's Board) discusses the company's long-term success this way: "...we built quality improvement and strategic planning on the foundation of servant-leadership. We became a community of powerful, trusting partners."

Undoubtedly better known than TD Industries, Southwest Airlines has in many ways revolutionized commercial air travel with its low fares, outstanding passenger experience, and relentless focus on efficient operations. The company is also known for a unique corporate culture that really does treat its employees as the company's most valuable assets—as perhaps best exemplified by the fact that Southwest executives are paid substantially less than their industry counterparts while Southwest employees are the best paid in the industry.

Herb Kelleher, Southwest's legendary co-founder and long-time CEO, is a strong proponent of servant-leadership. In the McGee-Cooper article, Kelleher says: "I have always believed that the best leader is the best server." Expanding on this idea, he adds, "Your employees come first. There's no question about that. If your employees are satisfied and happy and dedicated and inspired by what they are doing, then they make your customers happy..." In the same article, Southwest's former President, Colleen Barrett, adds: "Our entire philosophy of leadership is quite simple: Treat your people right, and good things will happen."

The results? In an industry where making a profit is notoriously difficult, Southwest has been profitable for 41 straight years.

So, does servant-leadership deliver results? In addition to TD Industries and Southwest Airlines—and Cleveland Clinic—many other organizations seem to think that the answer is yes. One list of more than 100 organizations that make specific reference to their embrace of servant-leadership principles includes such successful enterprises as 7-Eleven, AFLAC, The Container Store,

Herman Miller, HESS, Kaiser Permanente, Marriott, Men's Wear-house, Nordstrom, REI, Starbucks, and Toro[9].

Zappos, the immensely successful online retailer, is known for its outstanding **And then there's Zappos.** customer service and employee-friendly culture. Like so many of its Internet-driven counterparts, Zappos provides its 1500 or so employees with an easy-to-make-fun-of assortment of goodies:

We've got everything you can imagine: delicious bistro, coffee shop, yoga studio, nap room, gym, green-space backyard, rooftop deck, patio furniture, hammocks, ping pong, sand-floored beachy conference room, co-working space on the top floor with panoramic views and even touch screen video games in the elevators to make your ride up and down the 10 floors just a little more fun!

But it's not just about "fun atmosphere." Zappos has built its culture on the firm belief that what really makes people happy at work is their emotional connection to the organization's suc-cess—and their having the freedom and tools to contribute to that success. Speaking of the company's critical customer service operation, for example, Zappos' CEO, Tony Hshieh (pronounced Shay), says:

…we just ask our reps to do whatever they feel is the right thing to do for the customer and the company. I think [customer service reps] are generally not happy because they don't have control over the situ-ation, whereas at Zappos there's really nothing that a rep can't do so there's no reason to ever escalate.

And speaking of of the manager's role at Zappos, Hshieh says:

The role of a manager is to remove obstacles and enable his/her direct reports to succeed. This means the best leaders are servant-leaders. They serve those they lead."

Would everything about the Zappos culture work for other companies? I doubt it. But have servant-leadership and high employee engagement correlated with great performance at Zap-pos? The company does over $1Billion in annual sales, with over 70% of that business coming from repeat customers. That's pretty impressive stuff.

---

9   http://mdernservantleader.com/featured/servant-leadership-companies-list/

Need more evidence of how servant-leadership contributes to high performance? How about this? In their book titled, *Seven Pillars of Servant-Leadership*, James Sipe and Don Frick compared the return on investment of 11 publicly held, servant-led companies [10]to the 11 "great" companies in Jim Collins' *Good to Great*, as well as the pre-tax return of the 500 largest public companies in the US. Over a 10-year period, the servant-led companies significantly outperformed the others[11].

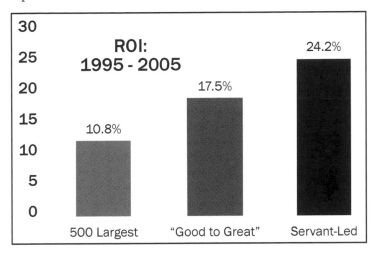

And of course, let's not forget that many organizations apply the principles of servant-leadership without using the label. *Inc. Magazine*, in an article called "How to Become a Servant Leader," once asked: "So if servant-leadership has all these benefits, why don't you hear about more people practicing it?" Kent Keith, the Greenleaf Center's former CEO responded: "…it's more widely spread than we know; people just aren't using the word servant-leadership, but they're doing what servant-leaders do."

For me at least, the jury is in, and the verdict is that the core principles of servant-leadership can help to create an engaged and highly successful organization. Listening to others, empathizing

---

10 Toro, Southwest Airlines, Starbucks, AFLAC, Men's Wearhouse, Synovus Financial, Herman Miller, ServiceMasters, Marriott, FedEx, and Medtronic.

11 Sipe, J and Frick, D. Seven Pillars of Servant-leadership. NJ: Paulist Press; 2009.

with their concerns, being committed to others' growth, leading by persuasion rather than coercion, having the ability to visualize and communicate a higher purpose—however you label this kind of leadership, I believe it has the power to transform your organization.

BUT WAIT!

Let's circle back to the question that opened this chapter: how do you create a caring/servant-leader mindset in leaders at every level of your organization?

As with any other major organizational change, the organization's senior leaders play a crucial role in its success by virtue of what they say, how they act, what they invest in, and what they recognize and reward. That means they have to take every opportunity to talk about what servant-leadership is all about—whether or not the organization decides to use that terminology. That means that your senior leaders will need to act like servant-leaders themselves. They'll need to reward leaders at every level who behave like servant-leaders and in the process achieve great results. And as an organization, you'll need to broaden what qualifies as "great results" to include helping others succeed.

In his best-selling book, *Give and Take*, psychologist Adam Grant talks about the differences between *givers*—those who put others' needs first—and *takers*, who put themselves first. Based on a decade of research, Grant also notes that, "Professionally, few of us act purely like givers or takers. We become *matchers*, striving to preserve an equal balance of giving and taking." Most relevant to our purposes here, Grant also suggests that, "If we broadened our image of success to include contributions to others along with individual accomplishments, people might be motivated to tilt...toward giving."

> ### Food for Thought
>
> The 2014 Workplace Bullying Survey found that 27% of Americans had suffered from abusive conduct at work. 56% of that bullying came at the hands of higher ranking individuals.
>
> How does your organization deal with abusive behavior?

Grant may not use the term, but he seems to believe that most people can be motivated to become servant-leaders. On the other hand, let's not be naïve. Those "takers" in your organization will not easily be convinced that they should lead by putting others first. Even if they can wrap their minds around the idea that this kind of leadership can help make the organization as a whole more successful, they will find it hard to change their ingrained tendency to be a taker. As we've said right from the beginning, change is hard.

So what do you do with these folks? You work with them. You encourage them. You reward them for taking steps in the right direction. You also make it clear that behavior that falls well outside the rough parameters of servant-leadership will not be rewarded.

Let me put it more bluntly: at the end of the day, leaders who can't stop bullying, backstabbing, and otherwise being abusive need to be shown the door, no matter how senior they are, no matter how successful they seem to be by some performance metrics. If that doesn't happen, their behavior will act like a drag anchor on your efforts to transform the organization. Once you do take action, it will send positive tremors through the whole organization.

Obviously, none of this is easy. But it can be done, and I guarantee that helping to make it happen will be one of the most satisfying things you ever accomplish in your career.

CHAPTER 13

CORNED BEEF ON RYE ... HEAVY
ON THE SERVANT-LEADERSHIP

ZINGERMAN'S DELI IN ANN ARBOR, MICHIGAN IS FAMOUS FOR its fabulous sandwiches, baked goods, and other goodies, but these days it also attracts business leaders from all over the country who want more than some great corned beef. As it turns out, there's a lot to learn at Zingerman's.

Ari Weinzweig and Paul Saginaw opened Zingerman's in 1982. Ten years later they had drawn rave reviews in the *New York Times*, *Bon Appetit*, and other publications; they were doing $5M a year—and they had hit the wall.

Searching for what to do next, they rejected the idea of expanding outside of Ann Arbor, for fear of losing control over quality.

After two years of thinking (and arguing), they published "Zinger-man's 2009," their vision for the future. The idea was to develop a "Zingerman's Community of Businesses" made up of a dozen or so small businesses in the Ann Arbor area. Each would have a managing partner with a share in the ownership. Each would be independent, but in some way designed to support the core mission of delivering great food and great service to the customer base.

The idea met with resistance from customers who were afraid the new growth strategy would ruin the Zingerman's experience they loved. It also met with resistance from managers who were afraid the new strategy would ruin *their* Zingerman's experience. According to Weinzweig, "People had gotten comfortable. We told them that we were going to have a significant culture change. It would be a lot like going back to a start-up. We'd have to work 90 hours a week again, and no one would be going home at 4 on Friday anymore. A lot of people didn't want to do that." In the next 18 months, 80% of the managers left the business.

> Has your organization hit a wall?
>
> Is there a way to tap into the talents of all your employees for a breakthrough?
>
> Where will the resistance come from?

Over time, however, the strategy worked. By 2001 there were 6 Zingerman's businesses, doing a combined $13M. Today there are 9 Zingerman's businesses, with a combined 600+ employees and $50M in annual revenue.

At the heart of this success is a commitment to servant-leadership. According to Paul Saginaw, "From the beginning, we wanted to build an extraordinary organization—not the biggest, not the most profitable—but an organization where decisions would not be based on who had the most authority but on whoever had the most relevant information. We wanted to invite everyone to help run the business and convey that each one of us was personally responsible for its success."

The company's website explains that "Servant-Leadership is, quite simply, the core component of our management work, the ingredient around which all our other recipes for leadership are configured." Not surprisingly, Zingerman's has developed its own unique way of talking about and applying servant-leadership. They've drawn from other sources as well, including the concept of "open book management." Every week, Zingerman's employees "huddle" in small groups to examine the company's latest numbers and discuss ways to make them better.

They've even built a very successful training business, ZingTrain, to teach the concept to both Zingerman's employees and increasingly, outsiders who want to sample the company's secret sauce.

To get a feel for all this, go to the section devoted to Servant-Leadership on the Zingerman's website[12]. There you'll find a wonderful discussion of the core principles of servant-leadership and the challenges involved in applying those principles, as well as Zingerman's "Recipe for Putting Servant-Leadership into Practice." To whet your appetite (Sorry, but I can't stop with the food puns!), here are a few quotes:

> *To live Servant-Leadership effectively, each of us has to really embrace the view that we come to work every day with the commitment to do what the organization needs done, to serve the entity as a whole even when that means that what we want or would like as individuals may get short shrift.*

> *Servant-Leadership creates paradox because it says that, although we hire, pay, promote and have formal authority over our staff, to the best of our ability, we are going to treat them as customers.*

> *Sometimes we, as leaders, have to choose to give up what we want for ourselves in the short term in order to provide more for others around us.*

That last point is worth commenting on. Treating your employees as customers means investing in them, which means spending money that otherwise would go somewhere else—not limited to, but quite possibly including, executive compensation. Over the years, Ari Weinzweig and Paul Saginaw could certainly have taken more for themselves out of Zingerman's, and paid their employees less. But as Saginaw points out, "Employees who are stressed out financially, wondering how to pay for their

Enough is enough.

---

kid's allergy meds, or their rent or auto insurance, are not going to be able to do their job well." And as for him and his partner, "We're comfortable with the notion that there's such a thing as enough. Others may be wealthier than we'll ever be, but I wonder if they've lost a certain amount of joy in their work."

Being a servant-leader probably does entail getting "comfortable with the notion that there's such a thing as enough." The executives at Southwest Airlines, who pay themselves less than their industry counterparts while Southwest employees are the industry's best paid, seem to understand that.

What if these various servant-leaders did *not* believe that sometimes less is more? Would their employees be as engaged? Would the companies provide the same level of service? Would their customers be as loyal? Would volume and revenue be as high?

In the end, would more actually be less? I really hate to put it this way, but isn't this food for thought?

CHAPTER 14

IF YOU WANT TO GET BETTER, YOU
HAVE TO TAKE YOUR MEDICINE

ONE OF THE MOST IMPORTANT LESSONS I'VE LEARNED OVER THE
years is that there's no such thing as bad feedback. You may not
always like the feedback you receive, you may not even agree with
it 100%, but if you want to get better, you'd better take it—and
take it seriously. Developing the ability to receive feedback is first
indicator whether someone is a servant-leader-or not.

I learned this lesson even before I started my career. My twin
brother Carl and I went to Northwestern, where we both played
linebacker on the football team. Playing in the Big Ten was a far
cry from playing high school ball in a small Ohio township, and
the coaches at Northwestern weren't shy about giving us some
pretty direct feedback. Let's just say that the feedback on your mistakes had a lot of hard bark around it!

Saturday was game day, Monday was film day, and at least at
first, I hated Mondays. The coaches had a saying, "The film does
not lie," and on film day everything you had done in the previous
game was critiqued in front of your teammates. My brother and I
had been pretty successful players in high school, but film days at
Northwestern made us realize that "we're not in Kansas anymore."
There were times when I was really grateful for the fact that we
were sitting in a dark room. But at some point, I finally thought
to myself, I've got to handle these sessions better or I'm not going
to make it through four years of this. That's when I adopted the

point of view that no matter how much hard bark came with the feedback, no matter how hard it was to hear, I was going to use it to make myself the best player I could become. That didn't necessarily make me love Mondays, but it helped.

Later in my business career I adopted this same point of view, not only to improve my own performance but also to improve the performance of the organizations I worked in, most of which have been service businesses. The purpose of a service organization is to provide great service to the customer—and the best judge of that service is the customer. Customer feedback is the only way you can find out what you're doing right and what you're doing wrong; it's the best tool you have to help the organization get better.

Here's the point I really want to make. If you believe that a great leader puts the organization's needs first, if you believe that a great leader defines his or her purpose as bringing out the best in the organization and its people, then feedback is critically important to your becoming that kind of leader.

I've known leaders who were so threatened by feedback that they didn't want to hear it and wouldn't accept it if it couldn't be avoided. I've seen leaders resist customer or employee surveys for just that reason. I think they were afraid of how the feedback might affect their status, their prestige, their image. It was about them, not the organization.

I'll be the first to admit that feedback can sometimes make me defensive, which is a normal human reaction. But the key is how fast we get over our defensiveness, how seriously we take the feedback, and how we work with it.

> How do you typically react to feedback?
>
> How long does it take for you to get over feeling defensive?
>
> When was the last time you asked for feedback? What did you learn, what did you change, as a result?

Like any skill, learning to receive and make good use of feedback can be developed. But it can never be developed if you don't go out and ask for that feedback. And it can never be developed if you put yourself before your people and the organization.

So it boils down to this. Want to be a better leader? Want to build a better organization? Get some feedback—and embrace what you get.

CHAPTER 15

WHAT KIND OF LEADER DO
YOU CHOOSE TO BE?

THIS BOOK IS ABOUT BUILDING THE KIND OF ORGANIZATION that brings out the best in people—the kind of organization in which people take the mission personally and consistently make the extra effort necessary to help achieve that mission. It's about engagement and what a difference it makes.

As you've undoubtedly figured out by now, this book is really about leadership, about what it means and what it takes to be the kind of leader who inspires people to become highly engaged. In my business career I've had the privilege of working with, and learning from, a number of such leaders. In my work with the Greenleaf Center for Servant Leadership, I've met and learned from many more. But long before I'd ever heard about servant-leadership, I was fortunate to experience that kind of leadership firsthand, as an athlete playing for two extraordinary coaches, two extraordinary men.

> What leaders have made a direct impact on the kind of leader you've become?
>
> What lessons did they teach you?
>
> How could you pass those lessons on to others?

The first was Dave El'Hatton, my football and wrestling coach back in Howland Township, Ohio. Dave loved to win, but he insisted on winning with integrity. Dave cared about his players, and he taught me at a very early age what it means to really care about others. He set the bar high, but at the same time, he somehow made us feel that we were capable of reaching these high standards of excellence.

I remember that when my twin brother Carl and I were in seventh, eighth, and then ninth grade, he drove us to Ohio State to watch the state high school wrestling championships. The arena seemed huge to us, and we were more than a little in awe. On the way home, Coach always swung by the university's legendary football stadium. When one of us finally asked him why we always made that same stop, he said he wanted us to know that we had the talent to play at a place like Ohio State—and if we got there he wanted us to know what to expect. He wanted us to feel that we belonged at a place like that. If it happened, he didn't want us to feel intimidated by the experience. He wanted us to feel that we had already been there before. His faith in us made us think in a completely different way about who we were, who we wanted to be, and what we might possibly become. I thought about Coach El'Hatton a few years later when Carl and I ran onto the field to play in our first Big Ten game, and I've thought about him often since then, as I've worked to develop my own leadership identity.

My brother and I elected to attend Northwestern University, where Alex Agase was the head football coach. Like Coach El'Hatton, Alex was tough, demanding, and brutally honest, but he treated every player with respect, whether it was the starting quarterback or a kid near the bottom of the depth chart. He cared passionately about winning, but again like Coach El'Hatton, he insisted on winning with integrity. He lived and breathed football, but he understood that his players were at Northwestern to get an education and insisted that we work as hard in the classroom as we did on the field.

Alex never put himself first. Witness the fact that a year after one of his most successful seasons—a season in which he was named National Coach of the Year—he volunteered to take a pay cut because the university was facing a budget crisis. Being around Alex was a living lesson in doing the right thing and doing it without being told or asked.

In the early 1940s, Alex had been an offensive guard at the University of Illinois, earning All-American honors as a sophomore, before transferring to Purdue, where he again made All-American. In his senior year he joined the Marines, and as a 23-year-old second lieutenant led his platoon into combat on Iwo Jima and Okinawa, where he was wounded. None of his players knew any of this until after his death, because he never spoke about those experiences—experiences that must have shaped his approach to life forever.

After the war Alex returned to the University of Illinois, where he earned All-American honors for a third time. After college, he played professionally for six years, winning three NFL championships with the Cleveland Browns, and went on to a successful coaching career that included being named to the college football Hall of Fame.

Yet, for all his success, Alex never, ever gave the impression that it was about him. It was always about the game, the institution he served, and most of all it was about his players. I'm pretty sure he never heard the term "servant-leader," but as I've said before, it's not the terminology that matters. It's the values and the behavior.

We all get to choose the kind of leader we want to be. What leaders will you choose to model yourself after?

CHAPTER 16

BUT WHAT ABOUT STEVE JOBS?

IF YOU BELIEVE THE RESEARCH THAT SHOWS THAT ORGANIZA-tions with highly engaged employees outperform their compe-tition and the research that shows that leaders who care about their people and treat them with respect are critical to building an engaged organization, then what do you say about the late Steve Jobs and Apple? I get asked this question frequently, although the "tough but successful" leader in question varies.

Obviously, Apple has been hugely successful. The company has revolutionized the consumer electronics market, delivered an array of breakthrough products, and built an iconic brand that creates customers whose passion goes far beyond terms like "sat-isfaction" and "loyalty." And then of course, there's the fact that Apple has blown the doors off its competition in terms of financial performance.

None of this would be possible if the people at Apple weren't a highly engaged workforce—if they didn't have that strong emo-tional connection to the company and its mission that makes them go to extraordinary lengths to help the company succeed. So Apple must have leaders who care, right?

Well, not so much. In the words of Adam Lashinsky, who has written an in-depth study of how Apple operates, "[Steve] Jobs' brutality in dealing with subordinates legitimized a frighteningly harsh, bully-ing, and demanding culture

Just because it worked for Steve Jobs....

at Apple. Under Jobs, a culture of fear and intimidation found roots throughout the organization[13]."

It's been widely reported that Jobs was a micro-manager, obsessed with even the smallest details. He imposed outrageous demands and deadlines on his subordinates and lashed out at subordinates who failed to meet the goals he set.

In his provocatively titled 2007 book, *The No Asshole Rule: Building a Civilized Workplace and Surviving One That Isn't*, Stanford Business School professor Robert Sutton felt compelled to add a chapter dealing with "...compelling examples of people who seem to succeed *because* they are certified assholes."[14] Naming Jobs as "Exhibit One," Sutton points out that when he entered "Steve Jobs + Asshole" into Google, the search produced over *89,000* matches. I think it's safe to say that Jobs was a long way from being a servant-leader.

How do we explain Apple's success under his leadership? One explanation might be that Jobs' abusive behavior was directed almost exclusively at a relatively small number of senior people and that the leadership model at other levels of the company was different. As Lashinsky's research suggests, however, Jobs' behavior seems to have fostered a "culture of fear and intimidation," not just at senior levels but at all levels.

Another explanation might be that the rewards of working at Apple overcame the negative culture, but there's actually nothing to suggest that Apple was or is more generous toward its employees than other Silicon Valley tech firms, where stock options, sushi in the cafeteria, and state-of-the-art gyms are par for the course.

My best guess is that Jobs' passion for delivering fabulous products and his ability to communicate that to the people at Apple overcame the other negative aspects of his leadership. In the words of one former employee, and critic, of the company, "Most workers [at Apple], no matter how simple their job might be, truly

---

13   Lashinsky, Adam. *Inside Apple: How America's Most Admired—and Secretive—Company Really Works.* New York: Grand Central Publishing; 2012. P.23.

14   Sutton, Robert I. *The No Asshole Rule: Building a Civilized Workplace and Surviving One That Isn't.* New York: Grand Central Publishing; 2007.

feel they are changing the world with whatever they are doing[15]." When the mission becomes a personal cause....

Is it possible for leaders to treat the people around them badly and still have a successful organization? I suppose the answer is yes, although I'm also pretty sure that because Steve Jobs could pull this off doesn't mean that most people can. In fact, I'm convinced that while leaders who treat their people badly may achieve some short term success, by and large they do *not* build organizations that succeed over the long term.

As Robert Sutton notes, in his chapter on Steve Jobs and other "asshole" leaders: "Sure, there are successful assholes out there, but ...generally, it turns out that companies can gain a competitive advantage by giving their people personal respect, training them to be effective and humane managers, allowing them time and resources to take care of themselves and their families, using layoffs as a last resort, and making it safe to express concerns, try new things, and talk openly about failures."

I believe that for most leaders, "If you don't care, they won't care" is still the best guiding principle to follow. As I've said before, we all get to choose what kind of leader we want to be. What kind of leader do you want to be?

---

15   See http://www.quora.com/What-is-the-internal-culture-like-at-Apple.

CHAPTER 17

NOTES FROM THE FIELD

NOT SO LONG AGO, CLEVELAND CLINIC OPERATED PRIMARILY IN command and control mode. While no one on the executive team would ever have put it in these terms, I'd say that the organization was seen more as a machine than as an organism. The goal was to keep the machine operating at maximum efficiency by keeping all the parts working individually and together according to a set of rigorous standards.

The lines of authority were clearly defined. Leaders at every level set the goals for their subordinates and monitored their performance. Subordinates were expected to follow the mandates of those above them in the chain of command. While most of the Clinic's leaders treated their subordinates with respect, it could hardly be said that they placed a high priority on "serving" them or sharing power with them.

The Gallup survey showed that the system did indeed give employees a clear sense of what was expected of them (a 4.4 out of 5 rating). But as we've seen previously, employees gave the Clinic significantly lower ratings on a whole array of other items: whether their opinions counted, whether they were recognized for their work, whether they felt connected to the mission, whether their supervisor cared about them as a person, or whether anyone encouraged their development.

The Clinic was (and still is) rated one of the country's best hospital systems, recognized not only for its clinical excellence but also for its operating efficiency. So in that sense the top-down, command and control approach seemed to be working. On the other hand, there was the troubling issue of the Clinic's far from great level of overall patient satisfaction and the related issue of low employee engagement as captured in the Gallup survey.

With all this in mind, the CEO, to his great credit, realized that change was needed, and when the idea of introducing servant-leadership at

Introducing Servant-leadership...

the Clinic was put in front of him, he agreed that it was worth exploring.

The next step was to win the support of the executive team. I didn't get much sleep the night before I proposed the idea of servant-leadership to the executive team, knowing that it would represent a huge change in how the organization and its leaders operated.

Maybe it was the executive team's dissatisfaction with the Clinic's poor patient satisfaction ratings, or maybe it was the fact that so many of the Clinic's executives are physicians, for whom the idea of service is embedded in their DNA, but, in any case, my basic argument, which went something like this, seemed to resonate:

A hospital is basically a service business. A world class service business depends on employees who will go the extra distance to solve the customer's problem. And while command and control leadership might deliver acceptable performance, it's not especially well suited to developing this kind of commitment and initiative. We can tell that from our own engagement and patient satisfaction scores.

So our leadership model needs to change. Some of the world's best service businesses practice some form of servant-leadership. Let's follow their example.

I closed my presentation by saying: "The servant-leader model may not be the right model for us. If it isn't, I'll find another, but I'm convinced that we

Food for Thought

In Good to Great, Jim Collins notes that "good-to-great leaders...got the right people on the bus, moved the wrong people off, and ushered the right people to the right seats."

Does your organization have the right people on the bus? Should some people get off at the next stop?

can't stay where we are and be successful in getting where we want to be in terms of engagement and the patient experience."

By the end of the meeting, with the support of the CEO, the executive team had agreed to move forward.

Of course, there was still skepticism. One key executive—not a physician, incidentally—was particularly resistant. While he agreed that the argument for servant-leadership might make sense in theory, he also felt very strongly that it just would not work at the Clinic. To borrow a medical analogy, he thought the Clinic's organizational culture would reject servant-leadership like the body's immune system fighting off an infection.

This particular executive never did buy into the idea of servant-leadership. Even after we had launched the initiative with some 400 director-level managers and were getting an enthusiastic response, he continued to believe that servant-leadership was incompatible with the Clinic's culture. As he put it in one of our more spirited conversations on the matter, "I'm not going to let you take 40,000 people down the wrong path." And while this disagreement was certainly not the only reason, it's probably worth noting that within a year he had left the organization.

ROLLING IT OUT.

In giving his support, the CEO noted that previous attempts to "mandate" large-scale change at the Clinic had failed. To build "pull" for the change he stressed that we should do a soft launch and "socialize" the idea of servant-leadership with managers at different levels of the organization before attempting a full roll-out—which is what we did.

You can't just tell people to become servant-leaders and expect them to get it. You have to help them understand what it means to be a servant-leader (again, even if you choose to use some other terminology). You have to teach them how to be a servant-leader and coach them and support them as they put servant-leader

> What's your teachable point of view?
>
> What do you think leadership is all about?
>
> What experiences and stories can help you convey this message

principles into practice. You have to speak from your own experience, your values, and your understanding of what the organization stands for and aspires to be. In other words, you have to draw on your own "teachable point of view[16]."

At Cleveland Clinic, I used the teachable point of view developed in many years of working with service organizations at Digital/Compaq and Blue Cross Blue Shield of Massachusetts to help convince my colleagues on the executive team that servant-leadership was critical to our success building an engaged enterprise.

At TD Industries, every new employee goes through an intensive one-day introduction to servant-leadership with three follow-up sessions, all designed to communicate why the organization deeply believes in this leadership model. Managers receive additional training to enhance their servant-leader skills, with regular refresher programs to ensure their continued development.

At Cleveland Clinic we brought in Third River Partners, an outside firm with specific expertise and a set of proprietary tools focused on implementing servant-leadership. Recognizing the importance of senior leaders in creating the conditions for cultural change, we began by providing servant-leader coaching to the Clinic's top 100 or so executives. This included a 360° servant-leadership assessment and a full year of SL coaching for the executive team. We followed that with a one-day servant-leader initiation program for some 400+ Director-level leaders, with follow-up coaching. To build a servant-leadership infrastructure across the enterprise, we then trained more than 100 servant-leader advisors to act as SL champions and coaches at the unit level.

Finally, to introduce the concept at the manager/supervisor level, servant-leadership training was piloted in several of the Clinic's Institutes and one of our regional hospitals before being rolled out across the enterprise. Within two years, all of the Clinic's 3000+ leaders had received servant-leader training. Today servant-leader training is built into the Clinic's leadership development program for all leaders from supervisor to executive level.

Once all of the Clinic's leaders had gone through servant-leader training, servant-leadership was integrated into the organization's

16   Tichy, Noel. *The Cycle of Leadership*. New York, NY: Harper Collins; 2004.

performance management tool. Leaders at every level now assess whether or not the leaders who report to them are demonstrating servant-leadership on a regular basis.

A whole set of servant-leadership tools was also developed, and 100+ senior leaders received extensive training in the use of these tools as well as the broader theoretical underpinnings of servant-leadership. Today these "Servant-Leadership Strategic Advisors" serve as champions and resources for servant-leader initiatives in the various institutes and divisions. They also meet quarterly as a community of practice to discuss SL best practices and ongoing projects across the enterprise.

I'm quite sure that at first some of the Clinic's leaders faked it. They may have thought that servant-leadership was some fuzzy-minded baloney cooked up by HR. But mindful of the organization's traditional command and control structure, they "went along" and "acted" like servant-leaders. Over time, I'm also convinced that most of our leaders did indeed move in the direction of servant-leadership. Why? Because our employee/caregivers told us so, in our Gallup surveys and more importantly in their behavior every day on the job.

Remember those items on the 2008 Gallup survey that received such low ratings from the Clinic's employee/caregivers? Whether their opinions count, whether they are recognized for their work, whether they feel connected to the mission, whether their supervisor cares about them as a person, whether anyone encourages their development? Since servant-leadership was implemented, those ratings have all gone up dramatically.

NEW ENGAGEMENT PROGRAMS

As important as it is for individual leaders to demonstrate caring on a relationship level, that's not enough. Caring must also be demonstrated at the enterprise level if you're going to create a truly engaged organization.

> What message is your organization sending to your employees with its programs and policies?

Over a period of several years, Cleveland Clinic's leadership team implemented an array of enterprise-level programs and policy initiatives specifically aimed at "caring for the caregivers." There's no doubt in my mind that those actions contributed to the significant increase in employee engagement over those same years.

Some of those initiatives affect a relatively small number of employees, but they've still had a significant symbolic impact. For example, the Clinic's Adoption Assistance benefit, which provides up to $10,000 toward adoption expenses, is used by only a few employees per year. Yet I believe having that benefit in place sends a message across the entire enterprise that "the organization cares."

The same is true for the Caregiver Hardship Program. Cleveland Clinic is surrounded by the working poor, many of whom work at the Clinic and do wonderful things on behalf of patients and their families every day. If they themselves need help to deal with a financial emergency, they can turn to the Hardship Program for a grant of up to $500. Fewer than 1000 Clinic employees per year receive assistance from the program—and $500 won't solve every problem—but for those 1000 caregivers and their families, it can keep the utilities from being turned off or their car from being repossessed. Having the program available sends a positive message across the entire organization.

And then there's the Clinic's Tuition Reimbursement Program: when the reimbursement amount was increased from the bottom 25% of market level to the upper 10%, the Clinic again sent a message to every employee that, "We care about you. We want and need you to keep growing, because you'll bring all that growth to the job you have today and the job you'll have tomorrow."

The Clinic also created a School at Work Program that helps caregivers earn their high school GED, which then enables them to compete for more desirable jobs within the Clinic or use the tuition reimbursement program to continue their education.

The initiative that has reached by far the most people is the Caregiver Wellness Program. For years the Clinic had reimbursed employees for the cost of certain wellness programs, but participation had always been very limited. Many employees couldn't or weren't willing to make the initial out-of-pocket expenditure. Work and family obligations made it hard to find time to participate. And then of course, there were the psychological issues that keep many people from even starting a diet and exercise program.

It seemed clear that a new approach was needed, which led to several questions. What if we offered our employees *free* access to Weight Watchers, Curves, and other wellness programs? What if we made participation easy by offering classes at our various facilities? And what if we even offered a small reward—say $100—just for taking that first step and participating?

The CEO and some other members of the executive team were initially lukewarm to the idea. Privately, and somewhat apologetically, one executive—who actually supported the program—explained, "This feels like we're giving something away, and that's not the way we usually do things." Others simply said, "It won't work."

Overcoming this resistance took many meetings and much discussion. The business case was important: healthier employees would perform better and also cost us less in sick days and employee healthcare. But the argument that resonated even more went something like this:

Ok, this is not *the way we usually do things, and that's exactly the point. People will see that we're doing something different, that we're making an investment in their health and well-being. That will send a message that we really do care about them. And it will give the whole organization a morale boost, which we can really use.*

At one point, despite all the discussion, the CEO and many members of the executive team were still holding back. Finally, out of frustration that I couldn't close the deal, I told the CEO, "Dr. Cosgrove, believe me, if we put this program in place, our employees will love you for it, and it will give our morale a shot in the arm." It may not sound like much of an argument, but I think it helped. Eventually he gave us at least his "conditional support."

With that support, the rest of the executive team fell in line and we launched the program—and was it ever successful! Twelve thousand five hundred employees participated in the first year (losing a total of 75,000 pounds). Over a thousand unsolicited letters thanking us for the program came in from caregivers across the organization.

As a footnote, the CEO was very pleased by the positive response. On more than one occasion I heard him joke that "It [the Wellness Program] is the only thing anyone thanks me for."

I was with him one day when a security officer quite literally gave him a bear hug while thanking him for the program and explaining how it had changed his life. Perhaps most important of all, as we developed ideas for other engagement-related programs, he often cited the success of the wellness program in giving his support.

Over time the program expanded to target employees suffering from a variety of chronic illnesses, and participation continued to grow. The medical results, and savings in employee healthcare costs have been dramatic. In the first two years after implementation of the chronic illness program, the Clinic saved approximately $78M in healthcare outlays for its employees.

Year after year, grateful employees continue to testify that the program has had a major positive impact on their lives and that it shows in a tangible way that the Clinic does indeed care about its caregivers.

WHAT ABOUT YOUR ORGANIZATION?

What works at Cleveland Clinic or Google or Southwest Airlines or Zingerman's may or may not work for your organization. You need to find out what *your* employees care about and come up with initiatives that speak to those concerns while being consistent with your organization's mission and business objectives. No matter what specific programs you decide to implement, it all comes down to caring about your people.

As I warned in the first few pages of this book, building an engaged enterprise takes time. Much of the change involved takes place behind the scenes—much of it takes place in the hearts and minds of the organization's leaders—and the results rarely become visible right away. That's why it's important to generate momentum and credibility with one or more highly visible initiatives, like the Clinic's Caregiver Wellness Program, that resonate strongly across the organization.

Even with success, you'll still encounter resistance. To keep moving forward, you'll need to keep making the business case for what you want to do. You'll need to keep connecting the dots between how your organization treats its people and how committed your people will be to the organization's success.

Especially in the early phases of your engagement strategy, when the hard data on engagement may not improve dramatically, you'll need to rely heavily on anecdotal data. You'll need to develop your own *Notes from the Field*—real life stories that illustrate how caring more for the people in your organization is making a real difference in how they feel and how they perform.

Look for those stories; tell those stories; celebrate those stories. Use all the communications tools at your disposal to make those stories a part of your organization's everyday conversation, and watch the needle start to move on engagement. But how do you keep the needle moving?

SECTION 4

OLD HABITS DIE HARD,
SO HARDWIRE THE CHANGE

CHAPTER 18

ORGANIZATIONAL CHANGE IS
A NEVER-ENDING PROCESS

OKAY, SO LET'S LOOK DOWN THE ROAD A BIT. YOU'VE IDENTI-
fied some critical areas of dissatisfaction in your organization and
tapped into them to build a compelling business case for change.
You've won buy-in from senior leadership for some new programs designed to satisfy some of your employees' most pressing
concerns and needs—and in the process you've begun to send a
message that the organization does care about its people. Most
importantly, you've nudged the organization somewhat away from
command and control and toward something at least a little more
like servant-leadership.

To get that far, you've done some very hard work. You've honed
your own "teachable point of view." You've fought some battles,
won some and lost some, in some cases put yourself at risk, and
probably made a few enemies in the process. And along the way,
you've had your share of sleepless nights.

You've made real progress. Your gut sense, as well as employee
feedback—formal or informal—tells you that engagement is on
the rise. Maybe you're even seeing improved performance that
seems related to the higher level of engagement. But here's the
question: how do you keep
the train heading down the
track? How do you keep the
organization from losing

> When you stop moving forward,
> you start moving back.

momentum and sliding back—because, trust me, there *will* be a tendency for that to happen.

HARDWIRING THE CHANGE: THREE KEY STEPS

Changing human behavior and sustaining the change is never easy. That's true for a dedicated couch potato trying to get in shape and stay in shape, and it's certainly true for a command and control manager trying to become a servant-leader. Those old habits die hard.

For an organization that's trying to transform itself into an engaged enterprise, here are three steps that can help.

1. HOLD YOUR LEADERS ACCOUNTABLE.

What could be more obvious than holding people accountable? Ask yourself—are the leaders in your organization held accountable for engagement in the same way that they're held accountable for other goals? Is it absolutely clear to the leaders in your organization that they need to focus as much on engagement as they do on other key goals and metrics? Does improving engagement have a high enough priority? If a leader at any level concludes that improving engagement in the organization will require an investment of time and money—time and money that could otherwise be spent on achieving another high priority goal—what is that leader likely to do?

Accountability requires goals and consequences.

You can't hold people accountable unless you can give them a clear goal and measure their success in achieving that goal. At Cleveland Clinic, every leader—from the supervisor of a small unit to the head of a major division—has an annual goal of improving engagement in the organization by X%, as measured by the Gallup engagement survey. Less comprehensive "pulse surveys," conducted every quarter using smaller employee samples, allow the leaders to track their progress—and adjust their efforts accordingly—on an ongoing basis.

In addition to measurable goals, accountability involves consequences. One of the most important steps in sustaining Cleveland

Clinic's successful engagement initiative was the decision to make engagement a significant component—40%—of a leader's performance rating. I remember very well how we arrived at that decision.

In the second year of our engagement initiative, when we looked at the results of the annual Gallup engagement survey, an interesting fact emerged. Every one of the more than 500 managers whose organizations had fallen into the bottom quartile on the survey had received an "exceptional" performance rating. In other words, the managers whose organizations were the worst in terms of engagement were still being recognized as outstanding leaders!

If we really wanted to raise engagement, it certainly seemed as if we were sending the wrong or at the very least a confusing, message.

It took much discussion for the executive team to come up with a solution. Ultimately, we made the rather dramatic decision that in the future, *40% of a leader's performance rating— every leader, including the members of the executive team—would be engagement-based.* We also agreed that any manager whose organization remained in the bottom quartile on the engagement survey would be ineligible for an "exceptional" rating. That would send a clear, unequivocal message across the enterprise that engagement was a high priority.

To make sure that our leaders had the support necessary to be successful, those whose organizations were in the bottom quartile in the annual engagement survey were provided with a coach who had specific engagement-related expertise and experience. Over time, some two-thirds of those organizations did in fact move out of the bottom quartile.

But what about the others—the leaders whose units remained mired in the bottom quartile on engagement, even with the benefit of time and direct support? In some cases they were reassigned to non-leadership roles. In some cases they were terminated. Some left the Clinic voluntarily.

Not everyone can be an effective servant-leader. Not everyone buys into the idea that "if you don't care, they won't care." Not everyone is able or willing to do what it takes to create an environment that encourages employees to become highly engaged. If people still don't get it, even after you've been clear about why engagement is critical and what it takes to build an engaged enterprise—if they can't or won't develop the necessary skills and mindset—you need to move them out.

2. CREATE ENGAGEMENT PLANS FOR EVERY UNIT, AT EVERY LEVEL.

In most organizations, it's standard procedure for leaders to develop an action plan to achieve their key goals. We're talking Management 101 here.

> Does your organization require an engagement plan from every leader, at every level? If not, why not?

At Cleveland Clinic, each of the organization's 4000+ leaders—with the help of an HR business partner—develops an annual plan to achieve the specific engagement goal set for his or her unit. Does this take time? Yes. Do some leaders view this as "one more thing I have to do?" Yes. But does it also help the Clinic's leaders and the people in their organizations think about what specific things they can do to create the conditions for higher engagement—and higher performance? Yes again.

Engagement is built mainly at the local level. Unless and until you get every leader at every level creating an engagement plan with the people in his or her unit, you'll find it very hard to get any traction. Is it worth the effort? How important is engagement to your organization? How important are the business results you hope to achieve as a result of great engagement?

3. RECOGNIZE AND REWARD BEHAVIOR THAT FOSTERS OR DEMONSTRATES ENGAGEMENT.

We all know how great it feels when someone says "thank you" for something we've done. In that moment, we feel good about ourselves, our connection to that other person is strengthened, and we may well feel motivated to be helpful again the next time we get the chance.

Given these natural human feelings, it's not surprising that recognition at work has been found to be a key driver of employee engagement. That's why Gallup includes "recognition in the past seven days" as one of the items on its Q12 engagement survey. It's also why a study by Watson Wyatt (now Towers Watson) concluded that "[…]manager-delivered recognition of employee performance boosts engagement the way a turbocharger cranks up a sports car's horsepower[17]."

> If your employees were asked to identify the one investment your organization could make that would have the greatest impact on their engagement, what do you think they'd say?

If you see your engagement initiative starting to pay off and you want to reinforce and sustain the progress you're beginning to make, find a way to leverage the power of recognition and reward.

A great place to start is by linking your leaders' performance ratings—and compensation—to their efforts to apply the principles of servant-leadership and increase engagement. As your leaders shift more and more toward a servant-leadership model, they will find themselves saying "thanks" more often to the people around them. To quote again from the Zingerman's website:

- Saying thanks is one of the key responsibilities we have as servant-leaders. Why?

- Everyone—you and me included—works more effectively when their efforts have been noticed and appreciated.

- Ultimately, saying thanks and recognizing people's contributions is one of the best ways to let people know that their efforts have really made a difference.

- It's a more effective and enjoyable way to work to be leading with appreciation than to lead with criticism

- When we say thanks, we set the tone to move our organizational culture towards a more appreciative, positive future.

In addition, you may want to develop a formal recognition program, which can be a great way to focus attention on people

---

17 *The Power of Recognition from Managers: Part 1: The Engagement Engine.* Towers Watson; 2010; New York, NY. Available from: http://www.towerswatson.com/en-US/Insights/IC-Types/Survey-Research-Results/2009/12/Turbocharging-Employee-Engagement-The-Power-of-Recognition-From-Managers-Part-1.

all across your organization whose actions reflect the organization's core values and demonstrate a high level of engagement. As we learned at Cleveland Clinic, the benefits of such a program can be dramatic in terms of the positive effect on the organizational culture and, in particular, on employee engagement.

CHAPTER 19

You Can't Sustain Success If You Don't Invest in Your People

I SPENT THE EARLY YEARS OF MY CAREER AT DIGITAL EQUIPMENT Corporation, which by the early '90s had grown to $14B in annual revenue, making us the world's second largest computer company behind IBM. Unfortunately, we failed to adapt quickly enough to the truly disruptive impact of personal computing technology. Despite our many strengths in both hardware and software, including the industry's first 64-bit technology, we found ourselves in serious trouble.

From 1991 to 1996, with our hardware sales in free fall, we were forced to make draconian budget cuts, including a reduction in force from 120,000 employees to 60,000. The only thing keeping us afloat was our service business, which transitioned from servicing only Digital customers to providing multi-vendor support, becoming the authorized, though invisible, service provider for companies like Compaq and HP. Despite the fact that our services division had become the company's profit engine, it was not immune to the austerity program. Not only did the division undergo substantial downsizing, but investment in infrastructure and training was also cut dramatically, to the point where customer satisfaction was affected. With the company literally struggling to make payroll, there was no other choice.

Ultimately we reached a critical decision point: to reinvest or give up the multi-vendor business because we could no longer meet those obligations. Recognizing that morale in the division was at an all-time low and that training in the latest technology was especially important to our people, Peter Mercury, the division's new General Manager, found the money for Digital on the Move, a global initiative that would deliver a whole array of new training programs and service tools.

Not surprisingly, many of our people didn't really believe that the company would follow through, so Peter and I (the division's VP of HR) went on the road to sell the program. In 6 months we traveled to 26 countries. Everywhere we went, people were skeptical. I remember a meeting we had with our team in the Netherlands, when an engineer stood up and said, "Sorry, but after these past five years, we just don't believe you." My response was, "I realize that right now there is nothing we can say to convince you we're serious about this. All I can ask right now is that you give us the benefit of the doubt and give us a chance to earn your trust on this."

Ultimately, we created a kind of discovery center-in-a-box that allowed leaders in every service region to present the Digital on the Move initiative to their people. Not only did the engineers attend, but other staff did as well, and even many of our customers. The message was clear: we were investing in our people. We were back.

The results were dramatic. The service division had conducted an employee satisfaction survey in 1996—before the decision to reinvest—and only 46% of the respondents had rated themselves as satisfied. In 1998, after the Galaxy of Initiatives launched, the same survey showed a 65% level of satisfaction. In that same year, Compaq and Digital merged, in large part because Compaq wanted to acquire Digital's field service capability. In the first year after the merger, employee satisfaction in the service division reached 78%. Over the next several years, Gartner, IDC, and Forrester ranked the combined global services division either #1 or #2 in the industry.

The point is you can go along for some time without investing in your people. Sometimes business circumstances leave you no choice. But in the long term, you can't succeed—and you certainly can't build an engaged enterprise—without making that investment.

Human nature being what it is, if you want to maximize the engagement return on that investment, make sure to let your people know about it. At Cleveland Clinic, for example, every caregiver has access to "My Total Rewards," an up-to-date online summary of his/her own Total Rewards package, including the current cash value of base pay, benefits, retirement, wellness programs, and awards.

As Peter Mercury used to say, "It's not enough to do good things for people; you have to remind them that you're doing good things."

CHAPTER 20

NOTES FROM THE FIELD

UP UNTIL 2010, CLEVELAND CLINIC HAD NO CONSISTENT, enterprise-wide recognition program. In June of that year we launched "Caregiver Celebrations," designed to give our leaders an easy-to-use tool to recognize outstanding behavior and performance in support of our core values. The program provides five levels of recognition:

1. *Appreciation—a non-monetary commendation from a manager, a peer, a patient, or a patient's family member.*
2. *Honors—a cash award of $10 to $100 presented by a manager to members of his/her unit, drawing on an annual award budget of $25 per direct report.*
3. *Excellence—a $250 cash award or gift certificate, plus a desktop award, given each quarter by the Divisions and Institutes. (Approximately 1% of the total caregiver population receives an Excellence award each quarter.)*
4. *Caregiver—50 awards of $2000 each year, plus a desktop award; 200 individuals are nominated from across the enterprise.*
5. *CEO Award—annually, 1 individual and 1 team are given an award of $10,000 each.*

Award recipients are highlighted in the Clinic's newsletter, on video screens throughout its many buildings, and at numerous events, including the highly publicized annual CEO banquet where the top tier awards are presented.

> Saying thanks doesn't cost much, but it matters a lot.

The preponderance of Caregiver Celebrations awards involves little or no money. Approximately 74% are "Appreciation" awards, simple thank you notes delivered via the Caregiver Celebrations website. The award contains a certificate and a short explanation of why it was sent and what company value was reinforced by the recipient's efforts. Another 23% are "Honors" awards of $100 or less. As a result, the total cost of the program is a tiny fraction of the Clinic's annual benefits budget. An independent review of the Clinic's total rewards system, including compensation and benefits, found that Caregiver Celebrations delivered a very high "bang for the buck" in terms of how much it was valued by employees compared to its cost.

Because it's so easy to use and so popular with recipients, Caregiver Celebrations quickly became embedded in Clinic's organizational culture. The average number of awards has increased dramatically since the launch in 2010, from 7500 to more than 19,000—per month! That's a lot of people saying thank you to a lot of people.

As for the program's effect on engagement, let's take a look at the Clinic's annual Gallup survey, in particular at this item: *In the last seven days, I have received recognition or praise for doing good work.* On the first survey, back in 2008, employees gave the Clinic a score of 3.24 on this item (based on a 5-point scale, with 1 being "Strongly Disagree" and 5 "Strongly Agree")—the lowest score of the 12 survey items. That score stayed essentially the same in 2009, but increased significantly inn 2010, after the launch of Caregiver Celebrations. By 2013, the score on that item had risen to 3.95— the largest increase in any of the Gallup survey items.

Does recognition drive engagement? Absolutely. Can a well thought out recognition program make a difference in your organization's engagement level? The answer is a resounding yes. Will you run into resistance if you propose such a program? The answer, again, is probably yes. If there's one thing I've learned, it's that even the best ideas will encounter initial resistance.

As with every other idea we've discussed in these pages, you have to build the business case. Remember that more than 70% of Caregiver Celebrations awards involve no money at all, and another 23% involve awards of less than $100. This is not about "buying love." And it's certainly not a budget buster.

What it is, is an investment worth making—if you really care about building an engaged enterprise.

SECTION 5

IT'S ABOUT BUILDING PYRAMIDS, NOT SANDCASTLES

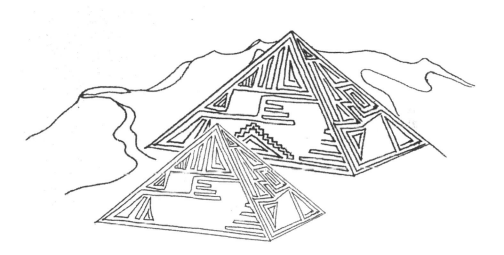

CHAPTER 21

CHANGE ALWAYS TAKES
LONGER THAN YOU THINK

ENGAGEMENT IS NOT ABOUT SCORES ON A SURVEY. IT'S ABOUT how the people in your organization feel about the organization and how they feel about the work they do. Ultimately it's about how they do that work—whether they do it just well enough to get by or they do it with that extra effort and commitment that makes the difference between ok performance and outstanding performance.

Assuming that this kind of engaged behavior is not the norm in your organization—which must be the case or you wouldn't be reading this book—it's going to take time to turn things around. For one thing, you probably have a significant number of actively disengaged employees—the people Gallup says "aren't just unhappy at work; they're busy acting out their unhappiness. Every day these workers undermine what their engaged co-workers accomplish."

You won't win those people over quickly, no matter what you do. And remember, according to Gallup it takes four engaged employees to offset the negative effect of just one actively disengaged employee. (In world class organizations, that ratio is much higher, more like 9.5 to 1.)

And then there's the fact that building an engaged organization means changing the way your leaders think and act. Even with the best of intentions and plenty of training, it takes time for any leader who has largely operated in a traditional command and control environment to add servant-leader principles to his or her leadership style. Because building an engaged organization involves such a major change in your culture, it will also require a multi-dimensional approach, with many different initiatives and programs and decisions—all of which takes time to unfold.

The problem is that having overcome resistance among your senior leaders and won their support for various engagement initiatives, you may find that they want results right away. If it takes time for your engagement strategy to show results—and it will—you'll probably see some weakening of their support. Patience may be a virtue, but it's praised more often than practiced.

Perhaps more damaging is that some of those political infighters who would like to see you fail (you know who they are) will feel emboldened. They'll use the lack of immediate results to undermine you and what you're trying to do. It only takes one or two of these people to do a great deal of damage.

If and when you run into this situation, you'll be tempted to back off. Don't do it. Instead, go back to the dissatisfaction you originally tapped into and remind everyone why engagement is so important. Make the business case again, and point out why it takes time to move the needle on something as complex as engagement. You'll get the support you need. You won't win everyone over, but you never get everyone's support.

If you use that support to keep moving forward, if your leaders at every level keep demonstrating that the organization does indeed care about the people who work there, you'll finally reach a tipping point. You'll start to see real results, as the balance between engaged and disengaged employees begins to shift.

I guarantee it: if you show your employees that the organization cares about them, they'll care about the organization. That will lead to a whole new level of engagement and performance.

CHAPTER 22

BEWARE THE BOOK OF SHOULDS

MY MOTHER ONCE SAID TO ME, "YOU KNOW, IF YOU LOOK AT the times in your life when you've been the most disappointed, it's when your expectations have not been met." As she was about many things, she was certainly right about that.

Sometimes I think that my biggest challenge in life, both personally and professionally, has been tied up with managing expectations—whether that involves managing my own expectations or helping others manage theirs. Most of us would be a lot happier if we weren't always struggling to achieve some expectation we or others have set for ourselves, or even worse, trying to deal with the disappointment and frustration that comes with expectations we've failed to meet.

What expectations are you struggling with at the moment? Are the issues personal: "I should be higher on the executive ladder by now." "I should be running a bigger organization." "I should be making more money." Perhaps the issues are organizational: "We should already have delivered that new product. Why can't our engineers get the bugs out?" Or, "We should own that market by now. Why can't we get any traction?" Or, "We've missed our revenue target for the third straight quarter. How do we get back on track?"

What's especially frustrating is that the expectations we struggle with most often seem to have come out of nowhere. Even when they come wrapped up in some rationale—this quarter's target is based on last quarter's, or it's based on an industry benchmark, or whatever—when you dig down, all too often the rationale seems pretty thin. Ultimately, the expectation just seems to come down to somebody's idea of what should happen. It seems to come down to the *Book of Shoulds!*

We all know that book. Even though it has never been written, we devote much of our lives to it.

There must be a chapter in the *Book of Shoulds* devoted to organizational change. Somewhere in that chapter it must say that change should always be happening faster, because in my experience, that's what most leaders think, regardless of how big a change you're trying to accomplish and almost regardless of how much progress you're actually making. The question is always: why is it taking so long for us to move the needle? When do we really start to get results? Why isn't this happening faster?

If you're going to resist the quick fix approach, if you're going to build a pyramid not a sandcastle, you'll need to reset these expectations and ground them in reality. There's a rule of thumb that when it comes to a major cultural change, it takes one year for every level of management between the CEO and line managers to fully achieve success. If your organization has four or five levels of management, you can expect it to take four or five years to build a truly engaged organization.

That's not to say that you won't see significant results considerably sooner than that, but it takes time to achieve lasting change. The pyramids were not built overnight.

One day while I was at Blue Cross Blue Shield of Massachusetts, I was sitting with Bill VanFaasen, the CEO, discussing people's perceptions of BCBSMA, and Bill said, "Joe, when I say Exxon, what pops into your mind?" Without thinking, I said, "Oily ducks." Bill came back with, "Joe, the Exxon Valdez oil spill happened almost 20 years ago, and today Exxon is actually one of the greenest companies in the world."

The point is that it takes time to change people's minds. It takes time to earn people's trust. It takes time to make engagement a habit and a way of life. Don't let the *Book of Shoulds* and its unrealistic expectations keep your organization from sticking to the plan. Keep doing the right thing for as long as it takes, and you won't be disappointed by the results.

One note of caution: many organizations will see an almost immediate uptick in engagement, just because they've begun to focus on it, and as a result they stop pushing ahead and move on to the next problem. What happens next? Progress stalls and the finger pointing begins. So don't declare victory too soon! Remember that it's about building pyramids, not sandcastles!

CHAPTER 23

KEEP THE SPOTLIGHT SHINING
ON ENGAGEMENT

RECOGNITION AND VISIBILITY GO HAND IN HAND WHEN YOU'RE trying to encourage and sustain certain kinds of behavior— engaged behavior—across your organization. While it's critically important to say thank you to the people who bring that extra level of commitment to their work, it's also important to share their example with others.

There are many ways to do it. Call these people out in meetings. Tell their stories in your newsletter. Let them tell their stories in short videos that can be shared across the organization. Hold recognition events across the organization on a regular basis. At Cleveland Clinic, a "rave wall" on the Caregiver Celebrations website lists the most recent 50 award recipients in each Division and Institute. At every meeting of the executive team, one recipient is invited with his or her manager to tell the story behind that particular award.

The important thing is to keep the spotlight on engagement. That's how you keep the idea of building an engaged enterprise from losing traction and fading away. It's not hard to do, and it's not expensive (although it does mean that someone in

> How does your organization keep the spotlight on engagement?
>
> What more could you do?

the organization has to make it happen). I guarantee that if you make the effort, engagement will "go viral" in your organization.

And wouldn't *that* be worth celebrating!

CHAPTER 24

NOTES FROM THE FIELD

LET'S TAKE A QUICK LOOK BACK. I BECAME THE CLEVELAND Clinic's Chief Human Resources Officer in December of 2007. In the spring of 2008, Gallup conducted its first engagement survey at the Clinic, and the results of the first Federal "HCHAPS" patient satisfaction survey were announced. The Clinic's poor showing on both surveys produced the dissatisfaction necessary to win executive team approval of a new engagement strategy.

In 2009 the Clinic launched several key components of that strategy—the servant-leadership program, the "we are all caregivers" campaign, and the caregiver wellness program. Then, in the summer of 2009, Gallup conducted another engagement survey. The result? Nothing. In fact, depending on how you looked at the data, we were actually in a slightly *lower* percentile on engagement than we had been a year before.

This was not welcome news. A number of senior leaders, including the CEO, made it clear to me that they were not pleased. We had invested in new programs, made a considerable splash with those programs, and had nothing to show for it. In response, I reiterated the business case. I pointed out that the individual programs were being well received—citing especially the high participation in the wellness program—and argued that it was only a matter of time before that translated into higher overall levels of engagement. I even brought in someone from Gallup to explain that these kinds of early (non)-results were very common. Ultimately, to their great credit, the executive team hung in there.

In 2010, we kept moving forward. Servant-leadership training was expanded; the Cleveland Clinic Experience Program and Caregiver Celebrations Programs were launched; engagement plans were developed by all 4000+ managers (and reviewed by our HR team); and engagement was embedded in the performance evaluation process for all managers. As all of these efforts came together, our scores on that year's engagement survey showed a significant increase. The needle finally moved.

Over time, the needle kept moving in the right direction. We went from the 43rd percentile compared to other hospital systems in Gallup's database to the 87th percentile. Our ratio of engaged to actively disengaged employees went from a dismal 2.5 to 1 in 2008 to a world class 10.5 to 1 in 2013. Most importantly—because engagement is really about better performance—our patient satisfaction, as measured by the Federal HCHAPS, improved in direct parallel to our engagement.

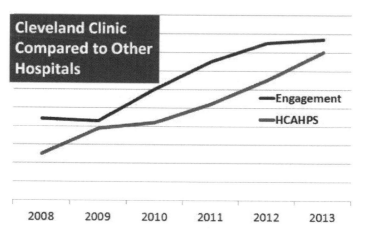

These results occurred during a period when the Clinic had to close down one of the hospitals in the system and when financial pressures led to two layoffs and two delayed salary increases. Even in the face of these highly stressful circumstances, our people stayed with us. We had shown them that we cared, and they believed us, even when tough decisions had to be made.

Let's say it again: engagement is about how people feel about the organization they work in, and as a result, how much of themselves they bring to that work. It takes time—and patience—to develop the kind of leaders and build the kind of organization that makes people want to become engaged. Transforming your organization into that kind of organization takes time. It's about building something that lasts. It's about building pyramids not sandcastles. But it can be done, and the results can be very dramatic.

CONCLUSION

CHAPTER 25

GETTING STARTED

WHEN I SPEAK TO PEOPLE WHO WANT TO TRANSFORM THEIR organization into an engaged enterprise, I'm often asked, "Where do we start? What do we do first?" Like most interesting questions, there's no simple answer.

Let's assume that you've done the groundwork. You've identified some critical dissatisfiers. You've built the business case that increasing employee engagement will help the organization improve its performance in those areas. You've won the support you need from other leaders—which means that you've managed to overcome at least some of the resistance you ran into along the way.

If the organization you lead is small—whether that means you're responsible for a small unit within a large enterprise or you're running a small business—the next steps are actually pretty straightforward, at least in principle. You start by listening to your people. Ask them what's bothering them, what would help them do their job better, what would make the work environment more efficient and more satisfying. Ask for their ideas of how to make things better. Take those concerns and ideas seriously. Fix the things you can fix, and ask the leaders with a wider span of control for help with the stuff that's "above your pay grade."

Make sure you keep your people in the loop. Be honest about what you can and can't do: they won't expect you to make everything better and they'll appreciate your giving it your best shot. That alone will get you started on the path to higher engagement.

If you make a habit of listening to your people and treating their concerns and ideas with respect, you'll see the results.

Of course, everything is more complicated if you're trying to change a large organization, with hundreds or even thousands of line managers, department heads, directors, and executives, each of them every day having their own impact on engagement. How do you get all of those leaders to understand the connection between engagement and performance—and get them to act in ways that over time encourage, rather than discourage, high levels of engagement? How and when do you start the conversation that makes that happen?

At Cleveland Clinic I came on board in the midst of a major strategic review. New strategic plans were being developed for each of seven key operational components. No sooner had I walked in the door than I was tasked with developing a new "people strategy" to deal with what many members of the executive team already recognized as the Clinic's serious employee morale problem. That opened the door for a high level discussion of what it would take to make the Clinic a "great place to work and grow," with high levels of engagement across the enterprise. That led to the decision to commission Gallup to profile our current engagement status, and those results—along with the results of the HCHAPS patient satisfaction survey shortly thereafter—created the dissatisfaction, and ultimately the support, that allowed us to launch the first of our key engagement programs: the servant-leadership, caregiver wellness, and "we are all caregivers" initiatives.

What if you're not sure that at the moment you have the political capital to support a broad-based engagement strategy? In that case your best option might be to start by focusing on a single program that will have an immediate positive impact on engagement and thereby create a positive context for a broader discussion of engagement strategy later on.

What about a recognition program like Cleveland Clinic's Caregiver Celebrations? Like most organizations, you probably already recognize employees for exceptional longevity or performance, so it shouldn't be too difficult to build on whatever is already being done. What if you expand the criteria for recognition, create a manager-friendly award process, and give the program a ton of visibility? If Caregiver Celebrations is any example, you'll see positive results very quickly. That might give you just the platform you need for a broader discussion of what it might take to really move the needle on engagement.

How and when you start that conversation will depend on your circumstances—but it's a discussion you'll have to have, preferably sooner rather than later, because no single program, no matter how popular it is with employees, is by itself going to transform your organization into an engaged organization.

> What program would make the best starting point for your engagement strategy?
>
> How can you sell it?
>
> What else will it take to win support for a broad-based engagement strategy?

CHAPTER 26

Engagement...What a Difference It Makes

<table>
<tr><td>

What stories can you tell about disengagement—and engagement—in your organization?

</td><td>

I'VE SAID IT BEFORE BUT IT BEARS repeating: engagement isn't really about numbers on a survey. It's about how people feel about their work and, as a result, how much of themselves they bring to that work.

</td></tr>
</table>

These stories, taken from my experience at Cleveland Clinic, speak to how disengagement—and engagement—show up in the everyday life of an organization. I'm sure you have some stories of your own.

JUST RESPECT ME WITH AN ANSWER

Management By Walking Around— MBWA, in management-speak—is thought to have been developed as a leadership practice in the 1970s at Hewlett-Packard. It got hot in the 80s after Tom Peters and Bob Waterman included it in their best-selling *In Search of Excellence*. The idea is that leaders should "walk around" to meet one-on-one or with small groups of employees on an informal basis as a

MBWA Tips

1. Make "walking around" a regular part of your day.

2. Go alone.

3. Talk less...listen more.

4. Always say thank you.

5. Never make a promise you can't keep.

way to identify problems, address concerns, and pick up ideas for improvement that they would never get otherwise.

I've been a believer in MBWA for my whole career. I think it's an invaluable tool for building engagement—if you really listen to what people tell you and take what they say seriously.

One of my favorite ways to practice MBWA is to eat lunch in the cafeteria. I go alone and almost always get involved in an interesting very revealing, conversation.

Not long after I joined Cleveland Clinic I went in on a Saturday to catch some of the people working the weekend shift. A nurse approached me in the cafeteria and asked if I was the "new HR guy." When I admitted that I was indeed that guy, he went on to say that his name was Frank and that he had worked the weekend shift for 15 years. In all that time, he had never gotten an answer to the question of why weekend nurses did not accrue personal days and vacation days at the same rate as those who worked during the week. He said, "I don't expect the policy to change, but I'd at least like somebody to respect me with an answer to my question."

I told him I'd check into it. When I asked about the policy the following week, I was told that it was a way to offset the increased compensation necessary to get nurses to work weekends. "Are we still having trouble getting nurses to work weekends, even with the higher pay?" I asked. The answer was yes. Then I asked, "Is it at least possible that the personal days and vacation policy actually dilutes the effect of the higher pay?" This time the answer was, "Well...maybe..." In the end, thanks to the Chief Nursing Officer's open mindedness, I was able to call Frank a few days later to tell him that we were going to change the policy. His response was, "I don't believe it. I really never expected to hear from you, never mind having anything change."

Employees understand that their ideas and recommendations won't always be accepted. When those ideas seem to just disappear into a black hole, that's harder to take. It sends a very clear message that the organization isn't listening and doesn't care.

So, if you want to show people that your organization does indeed care, the least you can do—in Frank's words—is "respect me with an answer."

15 MINUTES FOR LUNCH.

One day, when the cafeteria seemed to be especially crowded, a teenage boy wheeled his father, a patient at the clinic, up to the end of the long table where I was sitting. As he began to eat, the dad seemed upset by the fact that he was partially blocking people who were trying to get past him. Eventually he said, "They have a handicapped area over there, but the only people sitting there are people wearing badges."

I wasn't sure how to respond, but I had to do *something*. I said, "Be right back," and went over to the handicapped area. Sure enough he was right: all the tables were occupied by clearly un-handicapped hospital staff. Still not sure what to do, I began asking people if they realized they were sitting in a handicapped area, pointing out that people like my wheelchair-bound table-mate were having trouble maneuvering around in the main dining room. The responses varied. Some people started out by asking who I was—the unspoken question being "How is this any business of yours?" Some said they didn't know they were in a handicapped area—despite the obvious signage. Others seemed embarrassed and got up to move. One nurse indignantly said, "It's crowded in here today and I only have 15 minutes for lunch. If somebody with a wheelchair needs a spot, I'll move."

Were these people operating out of a strong emotional and intellectual connection to the Clinic, its mission, and its values? Were they putting "patients first?"

I went back to my table and invited the man and his son to move to the handicapped area, which they declined—although they seemed pleased that I had made an effort on their behalf.

SILENCE SAYS EVERYTHING.

On another occasion, I was sitting in the cafeteria across from two nurses, whose conversation I couldn't help overhearing. One was quite young, while the other, whose badge identified her as a Nurse Supervisor, was considerably older. The young nurse was saying that she could barely keep up with her patient load and that she worried about her ability to take proper care of so many patients.

The older nurse responded by saying that increasing the patient/nurse ratio was one of the ways "they" controlled costs at the Clinic. Then, in a more sympathetic tone, she added, "Look, I hate to say this, but you'll just have to get used to the feeling of going home at night knowing you haven't been able to satisfy all your patient's needs." That was followed by silence, and then they both got up and left.

I've worked in technology services, health insurance, and healthcare, and I'm convinced that one of the best ways to discourage people working in a service business is to make it hard or impossible for them to satisfy a customer's needs. Take away this basic source of job satisfaction, and you can say good-bye to employee engagement. Immediately after the new Chief Nursing Officer was hired she looked into the nurse to patient ratios and was able to take some aggressive steps to invest in hiring more nurses. This made a dramatic improvement in nursing engagement and patient experience.

FLOWERS FROM A VALET PARKING ATTENDANT.

For many patients and patient family members, a valet parking attendant is the first person they meet when they arrive for admittance to Cleveland Clinic. The attendants work for a third party vendor that handles parking on the Clinic's main campus.

This is the story of a young woman with a life threatening illness, her parents, and one of those parking attendants. Every day for over six months, the parents came to the hospital, as their daughter fought her personal battle. On most of those days they seemed to get the same young man as their valet parking attendant. Even if another attendant was poised to take their car, he would yell, "I've got these people."

Over time they shared their daughter's story with the attendant. Every day he asked about her, tried to be supportive, and generally made their visit to the hospital just a little brighter. One day when he asked about their daughter and they responded that she was near the end, and would probably not live more than another day. The next day the valet greeted them with flowers and a hug.

The family was so moved by his compassion and caring that they nominated him for a Caregiver Celebration Award. When they told their story and presented the award to him in front of 150 caregivers, I can tell you that there wasn't a dry eye in the house.

That's what it means to actually live the idea that "we are all caregivers." That's what engagement looks like, and that's the difference engagement can make in how an organization touches people's lives.

A FATHER SHOULD BE ABLE TO GIVE HIS DAUGHTER AWAY ON HER WEDDING DAY ... NO MATTER WHAT.

Holidays in a hospital are a little more difficult than other days. No matter how hard the staff tries, there's no hiding the fact that the patients and their family members would much rather be home and don't feel much like celebrating. On this particular Thanksgiving, however, the atmosphere on one floor was definitely different, as a young bride in her wedding gown, a young groom in his tux, and their entourage of attendants and family members swept down the corridor.

The bride's father had been in the hospital for months, waiting for a transplant that had not come. His condition was now terminal. A few days earlier, when it had become clear that the patient wouldn't live long enough to give his daughter away at her upcoming wedding, the head nurse on the floor called his family to say that the staff had offered to give up their Thanksgiving holiday so that the wedding could be held right there in the father's room. In addition to their regular duties, that group of dedicated caregivers also became wedding planners. They brought in flowers, food, and music; patients from neighboring rooms were invited; and a father was able to give his daughter away. The next morning he passed away.

You might think I made this story up, because it sounds so much like something out of a Hallmark made-for-TV movie. I assure you that it's true. There are many stories just like this one in hospitals all across the world, where people bring the best of themselves to work every day. While life and death circumstances may not be part of the routine in other industries and organizations, there's no doubt that engaged employees make a difference in people's lives, no matter what service they provide.

EPILOGUE: ONE LAST STORY

IN THESE PAGES I'VE TRIED TO PROVIDE YOU WITH A SET OF PRINciples that can help you build an organization where people bring the best of themselves to work, because they feel personally connected to the mission, feel empowered and equipped to do their job well, and believe that the organization's leaders, from the C-level to their own immediate supervisors, really care about them and value their contribution.

We've talked about how hard it is to create this kind of organization—about the challenges and the professional risk you'll face in taking on this task. We've laid out a few principles that can make the difference between success and failure and looked at a host of real world examples of what's involved in putting these principles into practice.

Most importantly, we've discussed the kind of leadership it takes to create this kind of engaged organization.

Now I'd like to leave you with one last, truly amazing story.

IF YOU CARE, THEY'LL CARE ... AND YOU MAY BE AMAZED AT HOW MUCH.

As I was writing this book, the Market Basket family feud was playing itself out in the board room, the 71 supermarkets, and the parking lots of this New England grocery chain. If you caught any of the extensive media coverage, you were undoubtedly as fascinated as I was.

According to *Fortune*, Market Basket is the 127th largest privately held business in the country, with 25,000 employees in 71 stores across Massachusetts, Maine, and New Hampshire, and $4B+ in revenue. The business dates back to 1916, when a Greek immigrant couple opened a small grocery store in Lowell, Massachusetts. In 1954 they turned the store over to two of their sons, George and Mike, who built it into a modern supermarket chain. When George died suddenly in 1971, all hell broke loose.

George's family accused Mike of defrauding them of their rightful share of the growing business. After 20+ years of litigation and other nastiness, the courts awarded them 51% of the company. After much more nastiness, spread over another 10+ years, one of George's descendants switched "sides" in 2008, enabling Mike's son, Arthur T. Demoulas, to be selected as CEO.

Since taking over the company, he has added stores, increased revenue, and, with reported margins in the 7% range, kept profits higher than most other supermarket chains. He has a strong sense that the business has an obligation to serve the communities in which it operates, and because of this he has also kept prices substantially lower than his competitors.

And what's especially relevant to our discussion here, he has also built an incredibly loyal workforce—with turnover far below industry norms—by offering higher than market pay, generous profit sharing and benefits, and according to employees, by "treating us like family." After walking through a Market Basket store with "Artie T," a columnist for the *Boston Globe* wrote:

> *Demoulas knew almost everyone's name. He knew the name of the guy cutting meat whose wife had just completed chemotherapy and asked about her with obvious concern. Customers came up to him and hugged him, cheered him on.*

Demoulas' management approach caused problems with "the other side of the family." They were particularly incensed in 2008 when he had the company put $46M into the profit sharing fund to compensate for losses in the wake of the financial crisis. According to media reports, they wanted the company to raise prices and take on debt in order to increase the payout to the shareholders; i.e., themselves and their families.

This brings us to the spring of 2014. The same family member who had switched sides to support Artie T in 2008 switched back, enabling the other side of the family (led by Arthur S. Demoulas, just to confuse matters a bit more) to again gain control of the Board.

It wasn't surprising that the Board then promptly fired Artie T. What *was* surprising was that the employees jumped into the fray. Thousands went out on strike; virtually all of the rest reported to work but also participated in demonstrations and wore signs at work supporting the ousted CEO. Many customers supported the protest, boycotting the stores and even joining with employees demonstrating outside the company headquarters. Soon most of the stores had become ghost towns with few customers and nearly empty shelves and counters.

For two months these non-unionized workers stuck to their guns, as Artie T pushed his plan to buy out the Artie S majority stockholders. With the company losing millions of dollars every week, the pressure mounted. Eventually Artie T's bid was accepted, the employees went back to work, and the company went back to serving its customers.

This is a complicated story, with more than enough blame to go around and plenty of room to disagree about business strategy. But it's amazing that ordinary employees would put their jobs on the line for a multi-millionaire CEO, citing how much he cares about them and how much they care about him, the company he led, and the customers and communities they serve. It's certainly worth noting that even with the company's lower prices and higher wages and benefits, it has consistently outperformed the competition in a very competitive marketplace.

As the *Boston Globe* remarked in its 2014 Top Places to Work issue, "If the Great Market Basket Protests of 2014 proved anything, it is that employee engagement matters. A lot."

How much of a difference would it make all across society if organizations like Market Basket were the rule and not the exception? What would it take to create this level of engagement in your organization? What could your organization achieve if you did it?

When are you going to start?

FAQS

IS EMPLOYEE ENGAGEMENT DIFFERENT FROM EMPLOYEE MORALE OR JOB SATISFACTION?

WHILE THESE TERMS OVERLAP CONSIDERABLY, THERE ARE DIF-ferences. Job satisfaction refers to how content employees are with their work environment, but it doesn't speak directly to the issue of performance. It is possible to have an employee be very satisfied with his/her job but not be a particularly high performer.

Employee morale is a broader term, in the sense that it associates job satisfaction with job performance. It's hard to imagine someone saying of their organization, "Our employees have really high morale, but their performance is lousy," or vice versa.

Employee engagement is a richer concept. It includes not only how content employees are, but also whether or not they feel a strong emotional and intellectual connection with their work and their organization.

Job satisfaction is an important, but not a sufficient, goal if you want to build an engaged organization. If your employees are dissatisfied with their working environment, they're not going to be highly engaged. On the other hand, if your organization has a high level of job satisfaction, that doesn't necessarily mean that it has a high level of engagement.

The important point is that in order to get the best out of your organization, you have to start by believing that there is a strong, direct connection between how people feel about the organization and how much they'll commit to its success. Keeping your employees satisfied or "happy" is nice, but it's not enough. In today's competitive world you can't afford to set the bar that low.

WE'RE A PRODUCT-DRIVEN BUSINESS. ISN'T ENGAGE-MENT MORE OF AN ISSUE FOR SERVICE BUSINESSES?

Is innovation critical to your organization's success? How about quality? Productivity? Sales? Customer satisfaction? The fact is that engaged employees make a difference in every business.

Many "product-driven" businesses have learned, often from customer/market feedback, that customer service (which is inextricably linked to employee engagement) is critical to the sales process, especially in terms of repeat sales. In many cases these companies have also discovered that customer service can be a critical contributor to profitability, and in some cases—think IBM—this discovery has transformed the entire business model. The bottom line is that even if you're primarily a "product" company, highly engaged employees can make a critical difference to your success.

WHAT'S THE BEST WAY TO ASSESS OUR CURRENT ENGAGEMENT LEVEL? CAN WE DO OUR OWN ENGAGE-MENT SURVEY OR DO WE NEED TO BRING IN A THIRD PARTY?

You can certainly collect informal, qualitative data on engagement in your organization by practicing some *Management By Walking Around* and by organizing some internal focus groups. As with any critical strategic objective, you need a rigorous quantitative measure of where you are today, both across the entire organization and in its various component groups. You need to know how you compare with other similar organizations. You need to measure change over time, on a regular basis, and you need to analyze the data in a variety of ways to understand what's really going on and how to adjust your efforts accordingly.

Especially for large organizations, getting all of this right is usually going to mean bringing in outside experts. Yes it will cost you money but it will be money well spent.

WHAT ABOUT OUR "MILLENNIALS?" IS ENGAGEMENT A DIFFERENT ISSUE FOR THEM, AS OPPOSED TO OUR OLDER EMPLOYEES?

Let's assume we're talking about employees born between 1980 and 1990. The research I've seen suggests that these folks are more likely to be highly engaged and less likely to be disengaged than their parents' generation. That's good news. But their most critical engagement drivers are also somewhat different.

Millennials place a very high priority on the opportunity to develop their skills and to be involved in interesting work—not years from now but right now. They prefer working collaboratively in a team environment. They make less of a distinction between their work life and their non-work life. This means they want more flexibility in how, where, and when they actually do their work. They have a very high need to feel that they are part of a socially responsible organization—that the organization they work in is interested in more than just the bottom line.

I suspect that for many organizations, millennials pose some new challenges. It's important to face those challenges because these young people have a great deal to offer—and they're the future.

Let's re-phrase the question a bit: will a one-size-fits-all engagement strategy work in an organization that has a genuinely multi-generational workforce? Probably not. But here's the thing: the basic principles of how to build engagement will still apply.

If you really care about your employees—including those millennials—you'll look for ways to address their concerns. You'll look for ways to help them develop to their full potential. You'll look for ways to help them translate your organization's mission into their personal cause. If you do all that, you'll get the best out of all your people.

OUR ORGANIZATION IS GOING THROUGH SOME ROUGH TIMES, AND WE NEED TO LAY OFF STAFF. IS THERE ANY WAY WE CAN DO THAT AND NOT RUIN THE PROGRESS WE'VE MADE ON ENGAGEMENT?

The first thing I'd suggest is that you make absolutely certain that a layoff is your only option. At Cleveland Clinic we were able on one occasion to avoid layoffs by providing an early retirement package.

I've also been part of a number of staff reductions. At Digital Equipment Corporation during the 1990s, as the company struggled to survive, tens of thousands of people were let go. My very strong sense is that while the people "left behind" were certainly upset by what had happened to their colleagues, they remained highly engaged.

Ken Olsen, the company's legendary founder, drove an inexpensive car, came to work in his L.L. Bean clothes, and loved to drop in unannounced to kibbitz with engineers about their projects. He invested in his people and supported them when they stepped out of their comfort zone. Even when the company began to lose its momentum, he resisted layoffs until there was no other option. This history of treating people well created a strong of sense of family and a workforce that was deeply committed to the company's success, which helped the company continue to do outstanding work even after the layoffs. I saw this up close in the Global Services Division, which built itself into an industry leader even after suffering through the same staff and budget cuts as other divisions.

As I mentioned earlier, at Cleveland Clinic we were forced to close one of the hospitals in the system, putting some 800 employees at risk. To minimize the impact, we provided ample notice of the closing and went to great lengths to explain why the decision to close had been made. We provided transition services to anyone who wanted them. Most importantly, we froze all "outside" hiring to give the hospital's employees first crack at new positions in the Cleveland Clinic system. More than 600 of the 800 employees, 75%, stayed within the system. Roughly 10% retired early.

During my time at the Clinic we went through two other limited layoffs, and in each case followed the same procedures. As a result, our engagement scores continued to rise all through these events.

Can you reduce staff without ruining morale and creating high levels of dis-engagement? The answer is yes—if you've treated people with respect before the layoffs and if you treat them with respect during the layoffs.

TOOLS & EXERCISES: PLANNING FOR SUCCESS

Whether you use these exercises to kick start your own thinking or as a framework for discussion with the members of your team, they should help you develop a customized engagement plan for your organization, based on the five principles for building an engaged enterprise.

I. WHAT'S YOUR LEADERSHIP MODEL?

This exercise will help you think about the leadership model you personally lean toward, as well as the leadership model that characterizes your organization as a whole.

Command & Control	Servant-leadership
• Position authority	• Moral authority
• Might makes right	• Puts others first
• Survival of the fittest	• Puts the organization first
• My way is better	• Empowers others
• People are tools	• Welcomes feedback
• The end justifies the means	• Builds consensus
• Who screwed up?	• Seeks solutions, not blame

With the above characteristics in mind, rate yourself on the C&C vs Servant-Leadership continuum:

Command & Control   *Servant-Leadership*
1   2   3   4   5   6   7

How do you think your people would rate you?

Command & Control   *Servant-Leadership*
1   2   3   4   5   6   7

How would you rate your organization as a whole?

Command & Control   *Servant-Leadership*
1   2   3   4   5   6   7

II. THE FIVE PRINCIPLES

1. IDENTIFY THE DISSATISFACTION: ORGANIZATIONAL PERFORMANCE

List the areas of performance critical to your organization. These might include *revenue growth, profitability, market share, customer satisfaction, quality, product development,* etc. Then apply the rating scales to identify the areas where increased engagement could provide the greatest benefit.

Areas of performance	Satisfaction rating: (On a 7-point scale from Totally Satisfied —Totally Dissatisfied)	Link to engagement: (On a 7-point scale from No Connection— Totally Connected)	Combined rating

2. IDENTIFY THE DISSATISFACTION: EMPLOYEE ENGAGEMENT

Drivers of engagement	Satisfaction rating: (On a 7-point scale from Totally Satisfied—Totally Dissatisfied)
Relationship with supervisors	
Opinions respected	
Employees treated fairly	
Connection to the mission	
Recognition	
Compensation	
Benefits	
Opportunities for development	

3. ENGAGEMENT INITIATIVES

In the exercise below, list any engagement-related programs or other initiatives that your organization could implement. Areas might include *employee wellness, rewards & recognition, leadership/ professional development, communications, benefits*, etc. To stimulate your thinking, refer to Exercise 2 above and the *Notes from the Field* throughout the book.

Engagement initiatives	How difficult / costly to implement: 7-point scale: No Problem— Very Difficult	Impact on engagement: 7-point scale: Minimal—High impact	Combined rating

Use the exercises above to build the business case for a new engagement strategy:

- Identify the areas of performance where improved engagement would make the greatest impact. Describe how and why as specifically as possible.

- Identify the issues in your organization that, if addressed, would have the greatest positive impact on employee engagement.

- Identify the initiatives that could produce the best "bang for the buck" in terms of their immediate impact on engagement. What would it take to get at least one of these initiatives off the ground right now?

4. IF YOU DON'T CARE...

Use the following exercise to assess your organization's leadership model.

Leadership behaviors	Rate Yourself: 7-point scale: Rarely— Frequently	Rate Your Senior Leadership Team: Rarely— Frequently	Rate Leaders Across the Enterprise: Rarely—Frequently
Puts organization first			
Sets stretch goals for self and others			
Personalizes the mission			
Connects mission to decisions			
Recognizes/raises visibility of others			
Seeks/values opinions of others			
Provides support & resources to help others succeed			
Focuses on strengths of others			
Seeks solutions, not blame			

- Lay out a timeline indicating the key actions your organization needs to take over the next 12-18 months to move the organization toward a "7" on the above exercise.

- Identify one program, initiative, benefit, etc. that your senior leadership could take right now to send the message that your organization cares about its people. What's preventing you from taking that step?

5. WHEN A MISSION BECOMES PERSONAL...

Assess your organization's mission, using the exercise below:

	Rate your mission on each attribute, using a 7-point scale:
Clear/compelling	
Widely understood & internalized	
Creates emotion	
Connects to everyday activities and customer needs	
Creates sense of higher purpose	

- How well do you think your *customers* know your organization's mission?

- Do they think you're achieving that mission?

- Boil down your organization's mission to just one sentence.

- How can you give the sentence more of an "emotional charge?" How can you make it more "personal" for your employees?

6. HARDWIRE THE CHANGE...

	Rate each system/process on a 7-point scale in terms of how well it supports/sustains engagement
Performance evaluation	
Rewards/recognition	
Talent acquisition	
Leadership/professional development	
Communications	
Executive dashboard	

- Identify one step that your senior leadership could take right now to make engagement more "visible" to leaders at all levels.

- What could you do right now to make leaders at every level more accountable for the engagement level of the people they lead?

7. BUILD PYRAMIDS, NOT SANDCASTLES...

- Identify one (or more) major cultural change or system implementation that would be widely viewed across your organization as highly successful? How long did it take to complete? How long did the leadership team think it would take before implementation began? What were the key learnings from that example?

- Can you cite a major cultural change or system implementation that took significantly longer to complete than expected? What were the key learnings from that example?

- Build an 18-24 month timeline showing which engagement initiatives you will deploy and when. Mark the expected "tipping point" when engagement should begin to show significant improvement.

III. A MODEL FOR ORGANIZATIONAL TRANSFORMATION

As you develop your engagement plan, you might use this well-known model to make sure that you're including all the necessary key components. Do you have the right people in place? If not, what will you do about that? Do you have the necessary development capabilities to train your leaders at every level? What about the underlying systems that enable your employees to feel that they have the tools to do their jobs right? Do you have an effective system to reward behavior that supports engagement? And lastly, how does your organization structure need to change?

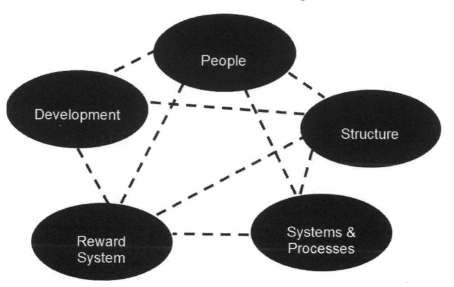

ABOUT JOSEPH M. PATRNCHAK
Principle, Green Summit Partners, LLC

 JOE PATRNCHAK IS HEAD OF GREEN SUM-
mit Partners, a consulting practice dedicated
to helping organizations bring out the best
in their people.

Prior to establishing Green Summit, Joe
served as Chief Human Resources Officer at
Cleveland Clinic. Tasked with making the
Clinic a great place to work and grow, building a highly engaged
workforce, and modernizing the HR function, he:

- Led development of a "we are all caregivers" culture—with
  innovative serving leadership, employee wellness, and recognition programs—that drove engagement to world class levels (as measured by Gallup), and contributed to a dramatically improved patient experience (as measured by Federal
  "HCHAPS" results).

- Implemented a new "people strategy" that transformed the
  Clinic into an employer of choice—recognized by numerous local, regional, and national awards.

- Directed deployment of HR best practices and a 21st cen-
  tury delivery platform greatly improved HR services.

Before joining Cleveland Clinic in 2007, Joe served as Chief
HR Officer and Senior Vice President at Blue Cross Blue Shield of
Massachusetts. At BCBSMA, he played a key role in reenergizing
this mature organization through new strategic planning, performance management, and leadership development processes, and
through innovative work-life, career development, and employee
health programs that improved engagement to benchmark levels.

Previously, Joe served as Vice President of Human Resources
for HP/Compaq/Digital, including leading HR for the $4.5B
Global Customer Services Division, which was cited for five years
by IDC, Gartner, and Forrester as the technology industry's #1 or
#2 service business.

Joe grew up in small-town Ohio, where he and his identical twin brother Carl were both multi-sport student athletes. At

Northwestern University, the two brothers served as defensive co-captains of the football team and were both named to the All Big Ten Academic Team.

In addition to his BA in Sociology from Northwestern, Joe holds an MS in Human Resources Management and Organizational Development from American University. He is also a graduate of the Advanced Executive Program at Northwestern University's Kellogg School, and the International Management Program at INSEAD, Fontainebleau, France.

Joe is active in a number of community service organizations and religious ministries, including serving as a Board Member of the Robert Greenleaf Center for Servant Leadership; Cleveland Inner City Tennis Clinics; Tenacity, Inc.; and the Oblates of the Virgin Mary. A co-Founder of the Healthcare Human Resources Forum, and a frequent conference speaker, he is the author of Building an Engaged Workforce at Cleveland Clinic (Journal of Healthcare Leadership, 2013) and Implementing Servant-leadership at Cleveland Clinic: A Case Study in Organizational Change (Journal of Servant-leadership, 2015), and co-author of Rewards, Recognition & Employee Engagement at Cleveland Clinic (Journal of Healthcare Leadership, 2014).

Joe divides his time between his Boston home and Vermont log cabin. He is an avid skier, tennis player, and fly fisherman.